# Who Governs?

# Chicago Studies in American Politics

A SERIES EDITED BY BENJAMIN I. PAGE, SUSAN HERBST,
LAWRENCE R. JACOBS, AND ADAM J. BERINSKY

*Also in the series:*

TRAPPED IN AMERICA'S SAFETY NET: ONE
FAMILY'S STRUGGLE  *by Andrea Louise
Campbell*

ARRESTING CITIZENSHIP: THE DEMOCRATIC
CONSEQUENCES OF AMERICAN CRIME CONTROL
*by Amy E. Lerman and Vesla M. Weaver*

HOW THE STATES SHAPED THE NATION:
AMERICAN ELECTORAL INSTITUTIONS AND
VOTER TURNOUT, 1920–2000  *by Melanie Jean
Springer*

THE AMERICAN WARFARE STATE: THE DOMESTIC
POLITICS OF MILITARY SPENDING  *by Rebecca
U. Thorpe*

CHANGING MINDS OR CHANGING CHANNELS?
PARTISAN NEWS IN AN AGE OF CHOICE  *by Kevin
Arceneaux and Martin Johnson*

TRADING DEMOCRACY FOR JUSTICE: CRIMINAL
CONVICTIONS AND THE DECLINE OF
NEIGHBORHOOD POLITICAL PARTICIPATION
*by Traci Burch*

WHITE-COLLAR GOVERNMENT: THE HIDDEN
ROLE OF CLASS IN ECONOMIC POLICY MAKING
*by Nicholas Carnes*

HOW PARTISAN MEDIA POLARIZE AMERICA  *by
Matthew Levendusky*

THE POLITICS OF BELONGING: RACE, PUBLIC
OPINION, AND IMMIGRATION  *by Natalie
Masuoka and Jane Junn*

POLITICAL TONE: HOW LEADERS TALK AND
WHY  *by Roderick P. Hart, Jay P. Childers, and
Colene J. Lind*

THE TIMELINE OF PRESIDENTIAL ELECTIONS:
HOW CAMPAIGNS DO (AND DO NOT) MATTER  *by
Robert S. Erikson and Christopher Wlezien*

LEARNING WHILE GOVERNING: EXPERTISE
AND ACCOUNTABILITY IN THE EXECUTIVE
BRANCH  *by Sean Gailmard and John W. Patty*

*Additional series titles follow the index*

# Who Governs?

*Presidents, Public Opinion, and Manipulation*

JAMES N. DRUCKMAN AND
LAWRENCE R. JACOBS

THE UNIVERSITY OF CHICAGO PRESS    CHICAGO AND LONDON

JAMES N. DRUCKMAN is the Payson S. Wild Professor of Political Science and Faculty Fellow at the Institute for Policy Research at Northwestern University and an honorary professor of political science at Aarhus University in Denmark.
LAWRENCE R. JACOBS is the Walter F. and Joan Mondale Chair for Political Studies at the Humphery School of Public Affairs and the Department of Political Science at the University of Minnesota.

The University of Chicago Press, Chicago 60637
The University of Chicago Press, Ltd., London
© 2015 by The University of Chicago
All rights reserved. Published 2015
Printed in the United States of America
24 23 22 21 20 19 18 17 16 15    1 2 3 4 5

ISBN-13: 978-0-226-23438-0  (cloth)
ISBN-13: 978-0-226-23441-0  (paper)
ISBN-13: 978-0-226-23455-7  (e-book)
DOI: 10.7208/chicago/9780226234557.001.0001

Library of Congress Cataloging-in-Publication Data

Druckman, James N., 1971– author.
   Who governs? : presidents, public opinion, and manipulation / James N. Druckman and Lawrence R. Jacobs.
        pages cm  —  (Chicago studies in American politics)
   ISBN 978-0-226-23438-0 (cloth : alk. paper)—ISBN 978-0-226-23441-0 (pbk. : alk. paper)—ISBN 978-0-226-23455-7 (e-book)  1. Presidents—United States. 2. Democracy—United States. 3. Public opinion—United States. 4. United States—Politics and government.  I. Jacobs, Lawrence R., author.  II. Title.  III. Series: Chicago studies in American politics.
JK516.D793 2015
320.973 — dc23
                                                                        2014026787

THIS BOOK IS DEDICATED TO JOHN TRYNESKI, EXECUTIVE EDITOR AT THE UNIVERSITY OF CHICAGO PRESS, WHO HAS DEVOTED HIS CAREER TO CONVERTING THE WORDS, IDEAS, AND RESEARCH OF SCHOLARS INTO KNOWLEDGE OF IMPORTANCE.

# Contents

Introduction   ix

**PART I.**     **Political Representation and Presidential Manipulation**

CHAPTER 1.   Presidential Crafted Talk and Democratic Theory   3

CHAPTER 2.   The Political Strategy of Tracking the Public   21

**PART II.**    **Presidential Strategies to Shape Public Opinion**

CHAPTER 3.   How White House Strategy Drives the Collection and Use
of Its Polling   43

CHAPTER 4.   Segmented Representation   60

CHAPTER 5.   Elite Strategies to Prime Issues and Image   73

**PART III.**   **America's Democratic Dilemmas**

CHAPTER 6.   The Effects and Limits of Presidential Efforts to Move
Public Opinion   97

CHAPTER 7.   Rethinking Representation   119

Acknowledgments   139

Notes   141

References   155

Index   177

# Introduction

A s the twenty-first century dawned, America faced new and serious threats to its economy and stature in the world. Al Qaeda's attacks on September 11, 2001, on New York City's World Trade Center and the Pentagon in Washington, DC, were unprecedented assaults and precipitated a series of momentous decisions by President George W. Bush—with support from congressional Republicans and Democrats—to launch what were expected to be short wars against Afghanistan (to deny a launching pad for terrorists) and, later, Iraq (to eliminate the threat of Saddam Hussein using weapons of mass destruction). By 2013, the wars had cost the lives of over seventy-one hundred Americans as well as nearly fifty thousand casualties (many quite severe) and run up a price tag of $4–$6 trillion—far above initial Bush administration estimates of $200 billion (Londono 2013; Iraq and Afghanistan Casualty Count, n.d.; Carter and Cox 2011). Despite the wars' high price, their outcomes remain decidedly mixed. Al Qaeda and its Taliban hosts were routed in Afghanistan, but experts worry that they are returning as US troops leave. Saddam Hussein was toppled, but the main rationale for the war (the existence of weapons of mass destruction) proved unfounded, Iraq is gripped by autocratic rule and instability rather than leading the "global democratic revolution" that President Bush anticipated, and, without Saddam Hussein serving as a counterbalance, Iran widened its influence and threat to American interests and allies in the Middle East (Friedman and Mandelbaum 2011).

Meanwhile, on America's domestic front, long-simmering and at times willfully neglected challenges burst into financial contagion in 2007 and would quickly decimate the economy in ways that experts compared to the Great Depression of the 1930s. With regulations weakened in the late 1990s or left unenforced over the next decade, home mortgages were

sold to millions who could not afford them in violation of financial guide-
lines, and, compounding the problem, these high-risk mortgages were
then traded among banks and other financial institutions under the false
guise of being safe investments. By 2007, conditions were in place for an
extraordinary economic implosion: the tightening economy prevented
vulnerable homeowners from making mortgage payments, which in turn
made it impossible for growing sections of the financial industry to make
payments on trillions of dollars of mortgage-based securities. Credit froze,
and banks and other financial investors lacked safety cushions that had
been a standard protection against poor investments. As 2008 unfolded,
a contagion started by homeowners unable to pay off mortgages spread
to the housing industry and started to infect a growing number of banks
and other financial institutions. As over one hundred bankruptcies struck
mortgage lenders and drained the solvency of the country's largest financial institutions—from Bear Stearns to Merrill Lynch and the insurance
giant AIG—the otherwise antigovernment and promarket administration of George W. Bush instigated unprecedented steps to prevent a "Herbert Hoover" catastrophe—as Vice President Richard Cheney warned
Republican members of Congress (Raju 2008). As the global financial
system teetered on the brink of collapse following the demise of Lehman
Brothers in October 2008, the Bush administration pushed through an
emergency rescue package—the Troubled Asset Relief Program—that
ignited both liberal complaints against bailouts of banks and conservative
outrage at the betrayal of small government principles, helping ignite the
Tea Party movement. The banking sector stabilized, but businesses and
consumers were rattled, pulled back on spending, and stalled the housing
and other sectors of the economy. For six months beginning in November
2008, more than half a million jobs were lost *per month*, and 5.2 million
jobs disappeared in the year after the crisis began in September 2008, producing the highest level of unemployment in three decades.

   As the economy nose-dived, the government's long-standing fiscal
mismanagement became readily apparent. Demands by conservative and
other lawmakers to cut taxes and expand exemptions for favored interests contributed to reducing the share of income that Americans paid in
taxes to the lowest level since 1958; the most affluent saw their marginal
rates cut to 33 percent or lower after having been about 90 percent from
the 1940s through the early 1960s. Meanwhile, the government's expendi-
tures rose as the costs of the Afghanistan and Iraq Wars came due without
new funds to pay them; Social Security and Medicare covered a growing
number of aging Americans who had contributed to the programs during

their working lives and lost savings in the financial crises; and the safety net kicked in to prevent millions from falling into deep deprivation owing to the sinking economy.

As America's quandary deepened and the scale of the cascading problems publicly blossomed, warnings sounded that the country was losing its global preeminence. Former Federal Reserve chairman Paul Volcker (2005) pinpointed "disturbing trends" in the economy several years *before* the financial crises that he considered to be "as dangerous and intractable as any I can remember." Volcker fretted about the "little willingness or capacity to do much about it." On the eve of the financial crisis, the former conservative strategist Kevin Phillips (2007) predicted America's "national decline" and compared it to the demise of earlier great powers, beginning with the Roman Empire. The National Intelligence Council (2008, 12) issued an alarming report that the "historic transfer of relative wealth and economic power from West to East . . . is without precedent in modern history," putting China in particular on track to have "more impact on the world over the next twenty years than any other country" and to make the United States "less dominant." Synching together the disparate trends, the *New York Times* columnist Thomas Friedman and the academic Michael Mandelbaum declared in 2011 that America is in a "slow decline, just slow enough for us to be able to pretend—or believe—that a decline is not taking place" (8).

Effectively addressing America's circumstances will require ingenuity and determination in the coming years and decades. Many are focused on diagnosing the economic and fiscal problems and identifying policy options, but little thought has been given to *how* authoritative figures reach decisions and attempt to lead the country. How we attempt to renew America will greatly affect the prospects of the country and its citizenry as a whole.

This book investigates the makers of America's national security, economic, and fiscal messes—our governing elites. The dominant view for generations has been that elites—specifically, the small set of individuals and groups who work in and around official government, including elected officials, civil servants, and policy experts—are the country's best hope. Insulating governing elites to operate as the deciders, it is claimed, allows them to exercise their extensive knowledge, broad experience, and wisdom to serve the country's best interests.

The doctrine of elite governance is comforting, yet America's most pressing challenges originate in poor decisions by the country's governing elites. Commentators and analysts disagree over what specifically went wrong with US interventions in Afghanistan and Iraq, but they do converge in criticizing senior government officials from Presidents George W. Bush and Barack Obama and their defense and national security staffs to members of Congress (Woodward 2006; Ricks 2006; Wright and Reese 2008; Gordon and Trainor 2012). The financial crisis originated, in part, in the decision of Bill Clinton to repeal the Glass Steagal Act, which was passed during the Great Depression to protect against bank speculation, and in the mistaken trust in the finance industry to police itself without careful oversight and regulation by the Bush administration and the Federal Reserve Bank under Alan Greenspan's direction (National Commission on the Causes of the Financial and Economic Crisis in the United States 2011; Carpenter 2011). Fiscal mismanagement has a number of sources, but most experts (including economists who worked for Ronald Reagan) point, in part, to President Bush's decisions to launch two wars and to expand Medicare without funding while at the same time enacting a series of large cuts in taxes that helped reduce revenues to their lowest levels in years.

The dismal record of governing elites in handling America's most urgent challenges has inspired skepticism about their ability among the general public and across the political spectrum from the conservative Tea Party to progressives (Williamson and Skocpol 2012; Hacker and Pierson 2010). Their track record of mistakes is too consistent and consequential to dismiss. It is time for a serious exploration of their behavior and motivations—what exactly do governing elites do, and why?

This book uses extraordinary new archival records to go behind the scenes at the pinnacle of American politics—the White House—to reveal what drives presidential decisions and political strategies. Our findings about the nature and orientation of presidential behavior have sobering implications for the governing doctrine of deferring to government officials that continues to hold sway as America seeks renewal. The details of today's fiscal, financial, and national security debacles have been investigated. What has not been examined adequately is the broader style of elite governance that contributed to America's setbacks. The target of this book is the long-standing presumption among many elites and scholars of American political institutions that government officials and presidents, in particular, pursue the national good—rather than the narrow agendas that they and their supporters favor.

Three themes emerge from our extensive research in presidential archives, interviews with senior White House officials, and examination of evidence that was either not previously examined or not subject to quantitative analyses. First, successive presidents from both political parties tracked public opinion to equip them to pursue sophisticated strategies to move Americans to support them and their policies. The White House's motivations, strategies, and tactics have concentrated on shaping and often misleading citizens in order to advantage itself and its supporters. Second, presidents claim to speak for "the people" and to serve the "public good," but we reveal the impact of narrow political and economic interests. Presidential appeals that tout devotion to country and the national good can be smokescreens to promote the preferences and wants of special interests and political insiders. Third, careful analyses of rarely studied White House records reveal the impacts—and limits—of the White House's persistent efforts to move Americans to support them. The cumulative effect of our analysis challenges venerable ideals of American democracy—presidents exploit the enormous and unrivaled capacities of their office to interfere with the legitimate efforts of citizens to evaluate them and to reach critical conclusions.

Our title—*Who Governs?*—captures our intent to penetrate the secluded backrooms of White House decision making and, through our reference to Robert Dahl's (1961) similarly titled book, the democratic dilemmas of elite governance. Few political theorists match Dahl's sustained attention to the possibilities of democracy to enable "people governing themselves as political equals" as well as to the reality that elites do most of the deciding and public talking on issues of broad concern (Dahl 1989, 341). Dahl reconciled the promise and limits of democracy through competitive, inclusive elections and a vibrant civil society that would equip citizens and check elites, building a valuable foundation for a nuanced analysis of presidential decision making and strategizing. Over the course of his career, however, he became increasingly impressed by the capacity of a broad spectrum of elites to short-circuit democratic representation by dictating economic and government policy. His sophisticated and nuanced exploration of the democratic implications of elite behavior and democratic practice invites empirically grounded and normatively alert research on presidential decision making. For all his contributions, it is telling that Dahl neglected a central feature of contemporary elite governing—the determined efforts of authoritative government officials to move public opinion to simulate "responsiveness," accepting the process of representation even as they attempt to shape the content of popular preferences to align with theirs.

Our investigation of presidents makes us (as it did Dahl) suspicious of pleas to leave the solution of America's contemporary problems to governing elites on the assumption that they are devoted to responding to "the people" and serving the country's collective good. The starting point for reevaluating how America makes collective decisions is the country's reigning doctrine of elite governance.

## A Myth: Effective Governance Requires Insulated Elite Governance

America's foreign policy champions the spread of democracy to the Middle East and other parts of the world. The reality, however, is that America's own founding explicitly rejected democracy in favor of a republic that would temper the input of citizens and insulate governing elites to make decisions that were expected to advance the country's best interests. The business and governing elites that gathered in a steamy Philadelphia in 1787 to pen the US Constitution were aiming to contain what they saw as "too much democracy" in the sovereign states that formed after the Declaration of Independence (Wood 1969; Beeman 2010). As James Madison declared in Federalist Paper no. 51: "The great difficulty lies in this: you must first enable the government to control the governed."[1] His particular concern was to contain what he feared was the "violence" of majoritarian movements and the mistaken or emotional judgments of everyday citizens.[2]

As democracy was feared as a source of intolerance, injustice, and dysfunctional governance, the "scheme of representation" was expected to elevate a governing elite that was educated, wise, and, able to "refine and enlarge the public views . . . to best discern the true interest of their country."[3] The Constitution sought to insulate governing elites to exercise independent judgment and action by creating a series of institutions—from the indirect selection of US senators and the lifetime appointment (without election) of federal judges to the creation of an electoral college that empowered each state to select, as Alexander Hamilton put it, "characters pre-eminent for ability and virtue" to select the president and free him from the "tempt[ation] to sacrifice his duty" to the demands of mass majorities.[4] Being shielded to serve as stewards of the people, presidents were expected to advance the country's overall, aggregate interests as the government's ceremonial head, commander in chief, and sole occupant of the executive branch. The Constitution's framers singled out the president as best able to "secure [the nation's] . . . interests" because of his unique ability to lead with "activity, secrecy, and despatch"[5] and to "act [on] his own opinion with vigor and decision" when "the interests of the people are at variance with their inclinations."[6] The US Constitution embraced, then, a doctrine of governance in which actual decision making was distanced from everyday people and delegated to their trustee-like representatives (see Bimes and Mulroy 2004; Gerring 1998; and Tulis 1987). And, as Edmund Burke famously declared in his 1774 speech to the electors of Bristol: "[Such a] representative owes you, not his industry only, but his judgment; and he betrays, instead of serving you, if he sacrifices it to your opinion."[7]

The US Constitution's deference to elites as an alternative to what was seen as ill-informed and intemperate citizen rule is a central motif in American political history and in debates about how the country should respond to its challenges. Writing in the turbulent period between the First and Second World Wars, Walter Lippmann warned that the public was a "mere phantom" or "deaf spectator in the back row" that "cannot be counted upon to apprehend regularly and promptly the reality of things" (Lippmann 1925/1993, 13, 77, 110, 198–99; see also Lippmann 1955, 20, 24–27). Government officials, Lippmann later lectured, "owe their private allegiance not to the opinions of the voters but to the law, to the criteria of their professions . . . [and] to their own conscientious and responsible convictions of their duty" (1955, 51). After the Second World War, Joseph Schumpeter (1950) derided everyday people for being distracted and detached and inclined to "drop down to a lower level of mental performance" on matters of public affairs. He recommended a form of technocracy in which elections are a "method" by which voters choose the deciders, who are then free to exercise their superior knowledge, experience, and judgment (see also Sartori 1987).

More recently, leading scholars of American political institutions have added their professional weight to the cause of elite independence from the citizenry. Some of these scholars have portrayed political leaders and presidents, in particular, as uniquely positioned to "ac[t] in the public interest" and to "pus[h] for leadership, control, responsibility, and effectiveness" and thus "fly in the face of . . . parochialism" (Canes-Wrone, Herron, and Shotts 2001, 536–37, 549; see also Moe 2003, 452–55). One prominent economist has suggested that better decisions would be reached by embracing the Federal Reserve's model of "technocratic policymaking" because it "stands above the fray, insulated from politics, making . . . policy on the merits" (Blinder 1997, 116–17, 125).

PART I

# Political Representation and Presidential Manipulation

### CHAPTER ONE

# Presidential Crafted Talk and Democratic Theory

D emocracy is the anchor of legitimacy for American governance. A large, varied, and long-standing body of political theory defined this notion of governance as a system of representation and, specifically, the vertical relationship between government officials and citizens and the institutional link created by the vote (for review, see Held 1996). Competitive elections, it has long been argued, motivate politicians seeking office or reelection to follow the policy preferences of the majority or the typical or "median voter" (Downs 1957; Mayhew 1974; Dahl 1971). The combination of a normative commitment to representation and elections supplies the building blocks for numerous empirical studies of "policy responsiveness"—the tendency of government policy to match the policy preferences of citizens (see Manza and Cook 2002a, 2002b; Soroka and Wlezien 2010).

The assembly line of research and theorizing on democracy is impressively productive, but it has missed fundamental realities of American politics and power (see also Disch 2011). The heart of the problem is that normative views about representation and rutted styles of analysis have clouded investigation of the actual process of representation and distracted attention from the ways in which the powerful in government seek to advance themselves by avoiding policy responsiveness and attempting to change citizen evaluations to avoid voter punishment.

Three fundamental research questions stand out. First, what is represented? While past research has concentrated on the *policy preferences* of the general public, elites strategize to widen their latitude on policy and avoid policy direction from voters. Policymakers do devote disproportionate attention to the select set of what voters consider *salient issues* (see also Burstein 2003). Although this heightens government attention to this subset of issues, it also narrows policy representation and relaxes the restrictions on decision makers regarding the large pool of remaining issues.

The policy representation described by past research is further constricted by the calculated strategies of politicians to prime the public to evaluate them on their *perceived personality* rather than just issues. Shifting the nature of representation from policy to nonpolicy considerations generates the potential for "shirking" in order to generate the political leeway from the risk of electoral punishment to exercise discretion to make policy (McChesney 1997; Bianco 1994).

Second, who is represented? Past research on political representation largely studied the relationship of government officials to the general public when in reality politicians are highly attentive to the demands of particular, privileged segments of the electorate with high incomes and other politically valued resources (Bartels 2008; Jacobs and Page 2005).

Third, how do politicians engage citizens? Studies of political representation often depict candidates and officeholders as agents who studiously comply with their principals in fear of losing reelection (King 1997). In reality, they treat public opinion as a movable object, not as a fixed threat. Political elites design sophisticated strategies to attempt to mold the public so that it supports them and their policies. Instead of genuine democratic representation, politicians engage in simulated representation—seeking to create the public opinion to which they respond.

This book takes a new approach. It closely studies the actual motivations and actions of presidents since John Kennedy to track and shape public opinion in order to spotlight theoretical and conceptual ambiguities and blind spots in past research on political representation. We weigh presidential approaches to representation against general questions about what and who is represented and how government officials treat citizens. Our findings suggest that presidents pursue a predictable approach to representation—including efforts to shape public opinion and direct their relationship with voters—that departs in significant respects from the notion of policy responsiveness that dominates research on US political representation (for a review of that literature, see Shapiro 2011).

Later chapters focus on archival and empirical research to investigate the White House's collection and use of its private polling data; this chapter moves in the other direction by inspecting democratic theory and empirical research for their general propositions about the nature of political representation by presidents. This chapter begins by critically examining the three questions at the core of debates over representation and then outlines our unique approach to studying them in later chapters.

## What Is Represented?

What elected officials represent affects their degree of freedom to make policy and chart a political strategy that advances them and their allies. Government that is responsive to citizens' policy views restricts elite decision making, while forms of representation that loosen the connection of policymakers to citizens create more leeway. Regulating the power of citizens is the project of elite governance and has fundamental implications for democratic legitimacy.

### Representative Democracy and Government Responsiveness to Policy Preferences

The dominant approach to American political representation posits government policy as "responsive" to the public's *policy preferences*—individuals' *directional* predilection to support or oppose a specific policy of liberal or conservative leaning (e.g., Erikson, MacKuen, and Stimson 2002). We refer to this type of vertical relationship that restricts government policy to what citizens prefer as the *responsiveness account*. Theoretical explorations of political representation pinpoint the "specification of the proper relationship between citizen preferences and the laws that govern them [as] the 'central normative problem' of democracy" (Rehfeld 2009, 214). Robert Dahl declares that the normative standard of American democracy is the "continuing responsiveness of the government to the preferences of its citizens" (Dahl 1971, 1; see also Pitkin 1967, 140).

The median voter theory reaches a similar conclusion; it predicts that politicians converge to the median voter's preference (Downs 1957; Black 1958). For example, as more Americans prefer that taxes be decreased, a left-leaning politician may alter his or her position to become more opposed to taxes. Politicians are expected to be motivated to adjust their issue positions—even those that are at odds with personal beliefs—because voters tend to support politicians who share their issue positions (Ansolabehere, Rodden, and Snyder 2008).[1]

The focus on how government officials react to the policy preferences of citizens also guides the bulk of empirical research on democratic representation, which compares publicly available surveys of mass opinion to policy decisions. "The connection between public preferences and public policy," Soroka and Wlezien (2010, 3) explain, "is one of the most critical components of representative democracy." This connection is inferred from evidence that the policy decisions of government officials or one of the elected branches correspond with the direction of public preferences for specific policies or general ideology. Until recently, most of the research on political representation reported evidence of high responsiveness and assumed one-way directionality—the causal flow starts with opinion and ends with subsequent government decisions (for review, see Disch 2011).

Despite broadly similar conclusions about responsiveness, research on political representation varies on the basis of the conceptualization of outcomes (dyadic or collective), the measurement of outcomes (e.g., spending and policy positions based on statements or votes), and the measurement of public opinion (from specific preferences for a particular policy to general ideological mood). Dyadic studies focus on the relationship between an individual representative, such as a member of Congress or the president, and the attitudes of his or her constituents. For example, Miller and Stokes (1963) conducted a seminal study that examined the correspondence between a House member's roll call voting behavior and the preferences of the voters from his or her district for positions on three policies—action on social welfare, support for American involvement in foreign affairs, and approval of action to protect civil rights. This dyadic approach spawned a veritable industry that generally confirmed the relationship between legislator behavior and constituency opinion even as it used new sources of data (Stone 1982; Powell 1982; Page, Shapiro, Gronke, and Rosenberg 1984; Shapiro, Brady, Brody, and Ferejohn 1990; Bartels 1991), improved statistical methods (Achen 1977, 1978; Erikson 1978; Hill and Hurley 1999), and intensively examined mechanisms that might account for responsiveness (Jacobs 1993; Jacobs and Shapiro 1994). The dyadic approach also expanded to consider the association of presidential budget proposals with public preferences regarding spending (Canes-Wrone 2006).

A second approach to studying representation focuses on the relationship between the public's policy preferences and system-level or collective policy outcomes (rather than the individual actions of representatives) (Druckman and Jacobs 2009). For example, Page and Shapiro (1983) examine thousands of policy preference survey questions, over time, and identify 357 cases where Americans' directional preference for a specific policy (e.g., level of taxation or military action) changed over time in conjunction with congruent changes in government policy (see also Weissberg 1978; Monroe 1979, 1998; Erikson, Wright, and McIver 1993; and Brooks and Manza 2006). Erikson, MacKuen, and Stimson (2002) compare a measure of collective policy along a continuum from liberalism to conservatism with a global measure of liberal or conservative public opinion (or "mood") that is based on aggregating more than fifteen hundred survey questions from 1956 to 1996. They conclude: "A shift in *Mood* yields an almost immediate shift in *Policy Activity*. . . . Like antelope in an open field, [officials] cock their ears and focus their full attention on the slightest sign of danger" (319–20).

### *The Political Construction of Representation: The Flight from Policy Responsiveness*

The previous preoccupation with government responsiveness overstates the degree to which citizen preference restricts elite discretion; it neglects important components of the practice of political representation. Political theorists question the authenticity of government responsiveness to authentic citizen deliberation. Jürgen Habermas (1989) derides what passes for "public opinion" as a "fiction" that "merely supplies acclamation" to elite exhortations (219, 238). Bernard Manin (1997) traces the shift from substantively rich parliamentary deliberation to poll-driven "audience democracy" in which citizens become passive receptacles for elite messages.

Research in coming chapters will investigate the possibilities and limits of presidential efforts to drive public opinion, as political theorists speculate. Our investigations excavate the tools and strategies of the White House's strategies to widen its policy latitude by redefining the nature of representation—to telescope the president's relationship with voters into a relatively small subset of issues that are salient and to recast his link to citizens from government policy to the nonpolicy dimension of personal image.

Presidents invest in extensive private polling in order to identify which specific policies are salient and then sink in still more resources in tracking the public's preferences regarding these individual issues. Their motivation to invest heavily in systematically collecting polling data on the public's preferences is to minimize the risk of alienating voters; this helps account for past evidence that politicians are "splitters" who respond to the public's preferences for specific policies (e.g., Canes-Wrone 2006; Page and Shapiro 1983; Manza and Cook 2002a, 2002b).

The detailed and resource-intensive tracking of salient issues generates discretion for presidents to fashion a less restrictive form of representation geared to the public's general mood. When issues lack particular salience, presidents capitalize on the leeway given them by a lack of close public scrutiny to broadly gauge the public's broad ideological leanings in conservative or liberal directions. This strategic orientation is consistent with past research finding that government officials act as "lumpers" who monitor aggregated public opinion for general ideological trends toward liberalism or conservatism (Erikson, MacKuen, and Stimson 2002).

What presidents represent extends beyond policy preferences, as previously studied. Modern presidents beginning with Kennedy increased their investment of financial and organizational resources in tracking the public's evaluation of the chief executive's personal attributes. The president's political needs calibrated which personal traits the White House tracked and how it profiled them. In particular, it routinely showcased positively perceived personality traits. For instance, after conducting "image polls" that reported the public's positive ranking of his traits of leadership and experience, Richard Nixon seized on his historic opening to China to showcase his skills in pulling off a daring breakthrough that projected American strength and national standing. The White House was also attuned to countering poor image perceptions—Nixon and his aides responded to his negative image for "caring" by orchestrating public activities and statements to spotlight his experience and competence.

White House efforts to highlight or bolster perceptions of the president as a strong leader embodying the nation resemble what the political theorist Hannah Pitkin (1967) describes as "symbolic representation" (see also Edelman 1985; Disch 2011; and Mansbridge 2003). This is a type of vertical relationship with citizens that depends on the president's ability to induce the public to believe that he "stands for" the country. Symbolic representation qualitatively differs from substantive representation along two dimensions: its form (appeals to symbols and alluring personality rather than policy) and the restraints on elite decision making (the leeway that flows from nonpolicy appeals in place of close government responsiveness to citizen policy preferences).

What is represented must become a central research question. Presidential strategies to construct the nature of representation suggest a concerted effort to widen White House discretion by narrowing substantive accountability to a limited set of salient issues and by shifting its appeal from government policy (the exclusive focus of most studies of political representation) to the nonpolicy dimension of personality traits and personal image.

## Who Is Represented?

Research on political representation focuses on whether politicians are responsive. This misstates the question. The central issue for representative democracy is, *Whom* do government officials respond to when making policy?

### Presidents Represent the Nation

Whom government officials respond to has often been equated with the "different modes of election," as Madison put it.[2] Legislators elected by local or state constituents are projected to serve these parochial interests, while the president's national electoral constituency is expected to motivate them to serve the overall public good. Woodrow Wilson (1908) built his scholarly reputation on his critique of Congress as overly particularistic and his lauding of presidents as the "one national voice in the country" (202). Summarizing the institutional approach to defining who is represented, Terry Moe confidently declares that presidents "addres[s] the needs and aspirations of a national constituency [while] . . . [legislators] are driven by localism" (2003, 425).

A number of empirical studies of political representation confirm the impact of institutions in melding representatives to their voting constituents. Miller and Stokes (1963) report the strong correspondence of members of Congress with the opinions of their constituents, as does subsequent dyadic research. Similarly, research finds that the president represents a national constituency, as he is expected to do (Erikson, MacKuen, and Stimson 2002; Druckman and Jacobs 2009).

Empirical evidence of presidential responsiveness to national public opinion fits snugly with median voter theory (Downs 1957). To win a presidential election, candidates and their parties are expected to lock down their base of support during the nomination phase and then concentrate their time and resources on converging toward the midpoint of national public opinion to capture the "swing voter" (Page 1978). In other words, the competition to win the median voter motivates presidential candidates to adopt policies that minimize the distance between them and most Americans.

The argument that presidents act as embodiments of national opinion and the public interest not only enjoys the backing of elegant theory and certain types of empirical research but is also embraced as a founding principle that is routinely broadcast by the mass media and the White House itself. But what do we know about why presidents take the positions they do? Accelerating changes in the structures of American politics and institutions are recasting political calculations and those whom presidents represent in practice.

## Segmented Representation

Political representation in the real world is not a fixed thing but changes as established legal structures interact with the struggle for institutional position and changes in incentive systems. In contemporary American politics, the elevation of party activists and single-issue advocates in the process of recruiting candidates and selecting each party's nominees has recalibrated political motivations regarding who is represented. In particular, the changed political structure has made it costly for politicians to compromise policy goals strongly held by activists, campaign contributors, and other allies in order to pursue centrist opinion as the median voter theory expects (McCarty, Poole, and Rosenthal 2005; Wood 2009).

Recent changes in the incentive structure of American politics have revived attention to bias in representation and, in particular, the disproportionate influence of party activists, the well organized, and the most affluent (Jacobs and Skocpol 2005a, 2005b). Bartels (2008) relates the roll call votes cast by US senators in the late 1980s and early 1990s to the policy views of their constituents and finds that constituents in the bottom third of the income distribution had *no* discernible impact on their senators' voting patterns while those in the upper third were quite influential. Gilens (2012) pursues a different research design and finds a comparable pattern of unequal responsiveness to the policy preferences of rich and poor citizens. Jacobs and Page's (2005) findings of government responsiveness to labor and, especially, business rather than the general public are further evidence of segmented responsiveness.

The government's responsiveness to the affluent often meshes with its attentiveness to the party faithful and to their liberal and conservative philosophical dispositions (West 1988; G. C. Wright 1989). B. Dan Wood

(2009) finds that presidents respond to ideologically oriented partisans rather than to the median voter and broad public opinion for two principal reasons: the high probability of reward in the form of volunteers and contributions and the near certainty of significant and enduring political punishment for policy compromise. Winning requires presidents to run as candidates of the Left or the Right and then to govern with clear liberal or conservative orientations. The political consequences of these systemic changes were on full display as George W. Bush pursued the agendas of economic conservatives who favored privatizing Social Security and enacting steep tax cuts for the affluent as well as social conservatives who cheered his stand for constitutionally banning gay marriage; his successor was cheered by Democrats and liberals for enacting national health insurance and a historic expansion of financial regulations (Skocpol and Jacobs 2011, 2012; Jacobs and Skocpol 2012).

Put simply, what is rational in American politics has been redefined. While the median voter theory predicted responsiveness to majority opinion, the polarization of elites and voters has motivated politicians to advance their careers by abiding by the policy goals favored by party activists, contributors, and others. Compromising these goals can be costly, generating primary challengers and a decline in campaign contributions (Wood 2009; Jacobs and Shapiro 2000).

The systemic changes in the institutions and incentives of American politics provoked the White House—beginning with FDR and accelerating under Nixon and, especially, Reagan—to recalibrate polling from tracking the general public to monitoring politically valued segments of the electorate. While the White House continued to track general public attitudes toward approval of the president and his policies, it also tracked and analyzed critical undecided voters who swing elections and indispensable components of the president's partisan base, loyal demographic clusters (such as the affluent), and philosophical soul mates.

Segmented representation is connected to the earlier consideration of what presidents represent—the White House's narrowing of policy responsiveness to the small set of salient issues and recasting of representation to personal image. Segmented representation requires presidents to "shirk" to create leeway on policy issues that enables them to respond to party activists and other core coalition partners (McChesney 1997). The overall effect is to diminish the White House's attention to the broader public and its policy preferences.

In short, the mistake of current research on political representation is to focus the investigation of government responsiveness on the public's policy preferences. The reality is that on many issues politicians, and presidents in particular, are responsive, but less to general public opinion (as much empirical representation research assumes), and more to party activists, philosophical sympathizers, favored demographic groups, and allied lobbyists and donors. Madison's presumption that their particular mode of election would predispose presidents to represent the nation as a whole has been conditioned or perhaps trumped by intense demands from well-organized particularistic groups.

## How Do Politicians Engage Citizens?

The responsiveness account portrays citizens as stern principals that timid agents (i.e., politicians) comply with if they do not wish to face the brutal punishment meted out to inattentive "antelope" (Erikson, MacKuen, and Stimson 2002; King 1997). Our direct knowledge, however, of the actual motivations of government officials is surprisingly slight given the vast warehouse of research on elections and political representation. Whether politicians are compliant agents is generally inferred from aggregate analyses. Neglected is the possibility of strategic agents who seek to change public attitudes or shirk the scrutiny of voters. Are presidents' compliant agents or strategic shirkers?

### The Presidential Inclination to Shape Public Opinion

White House archival records consistently reveal a president that attempts to move public opinion in order to minimize the risk of electoral punishment for pursuing the intensely held policy goals of the well-organized, the affluent, and party activists. Presidents enjoy asymmetrical advantages that allow them to conduct sustained, pinpointed, and institutionally equipped campaigns to shape and guide public attitudes in ways that serve their strategic interests.

Presidents alone can routinely communicate with the country through nationally televised addresses—most famously, the State of the Union speech—as well as daily public statements that are obsequiously reported by their own "media beat" campout at the White House or wherever they are traveling. They combine their unrivaled access to the media with their extraordinary institutional resources to attempt to shape mass communications and Americans' attitudes (Jacobs 1993; Jacobs and Shapiro 1995b). The Executive Office of the President equips the White House with the specialized staff, professional facilities, and routinized operations to merge sophisticated public opinion research with the skillful crafting and broad dissemination of the president's messages.

Before modern presidents speak publicly, private White House polling has often pinpointed the particular topics, words, and framings that resonate with existing attitudes in order to increase the probability of changing public opinion in desired ways. Changing incentive structures have interacted with institutional changes within the presidency to recast the representative relationship, boosting the White House's confidence that it can elude electoral punishment by eluding public scrutiny or by changing public opinion to support its policy goals.

## Presidential Strategies to Prime and Persuade Americans

As presidents devote their institutional and personal resources to moving public opinion, how much success will they enjoy in producing the public support they seek? For many years, the paucity of quality research on the impact of political communications on public opinion was "one of the most notable embarrassments of modern social science" (Bartels 1993, 267). Recent research, however, has produced a growing body of evidence of elite impact on public opinion as well as new concepts and research designs to trace both the mechanisms and conditions of these opinion changes and the media's intervening effects (e.g., Sniderman, Brody, and Tetlock 1991; Zaller 1992; Kinder 1998; Druckman and Lupia 2000; Chong and Druckman 2010; Iyengar 2010, 190).

Despite improvements in the analysis of *public opinion formation*, we continue to know little about the *intentional strategies of elites* to have these effects. Research on public opinion suggests two distinct, plausible approaches to moving citizen attitudes—first, priming or framing and, second, policy manipulation (on the equivalency of priming and framing in political communication research, see Druckman, Kuklinski, and Sigelman [2009]).

The first is the process of priming, which regulates the emphasis that individuals place on the importance of a policy issue or personality trait. Political candidates or government officials in authoritative positions may promote themselves by altering the salience of particular issues or traits—elevating the weight or importance that the public assigns to them as it forms evaluations (Enelow and Hinich 1984; Nelson and Oxley 1999; Druckman and Lupia 2006; Chong and Druckman 2007). The objective is to elevate the visibility of one issue over another (successful foreign policy over a struggling economy) or to supplant attention to divisive policies (say, unpopular wars) with personal traits such as daring leadership. In addition, a growing body of research in political psychology shows that individuals can also be steered by how choices are framed—public evaluation of a protest, for instance, flips if the protest is described as demonstrating free speech as compared to disrupting social order (for review, see Druckman 2011).

The strategic aim of political elites in pursuing priming (or framing) is not to directly change a voter's attitude on a particular issue—such as converting a tax opponent to a tax supporter—but rather to affect the level of importance the voter assigns an issue or how he or she understands that issue. Priming relies on activating existing and well-formed beliefs and attitudes (e.g., Chong and Druckman 2011).

The second approach political elites use to move public opinion is policy manipulation—persuading individuals to support the particular policies they favor even when real-world circumstances might reasonably lead to different conclusions. There is a long-standing fear—plainly evident in the Federalist Papers—that political elites and presidents can mold (or "demagogue") the public to adopt their policy views (Tulis 1987). Herman and Chomsky (1988) also warn that the public can be "manufactured"—though by powerful economic interests and owners of the media. We treat persuasion as a potential form of manipulation because public attitudes change; priming is a more subtle process of elite influence with less-enduring effects (see Druckman, Fein, and Leeper 2012; Chong and Druckman 2010).

Unfortunately, little is known about why and how political elites and authoritative leaders like presidents attempt to routinely move public opinion. Do they rely on manipulating policy preferences or on the more subtle processes of priming? Poor understanding of elite efforts to move public opinion raises significant questions about existing empirical research and democratic theory. Are government officials able to manufacture public support for their policies and, thereby, simulate the responsiveness detected by empirical research?

*Potential Effects and Conditions of Elite Efforts to Move Public Opinion*

Although ample research shows that campaigns, politicians, and the media influence public opinion (e.g., Zaller 1992; Gabel and Scheve 2007; Bullock 2011), we know little about the effects of deliberate elite strategies and tend to overlook a crucial distinction—elite intent to mold citizens and the actual effects of the attempt. Elites may fail to change opinion as they intend. Conversely, opinion may change in reaction to elites but not in the intended directions. Even partial answers to these possibilities would have enormous implications for empirical research and democratic theory related to political representation.

What research that does exist finds that presidential aspirations consistently fall far short of elite expectations. For instance, George Edwards finds a steady pattern of presidents failing to achieve their objectives of higher approval ratings or support for their policies (1996a, 1996b, 2003, 2007). Reviews of "minimal effects" research confirm Edwards's conclusion (Tedin, Rottinghaus, and Rodgers 2011; Cameron and Park 2011).

Even this limited research falls short, however, on several counts. It fails to compare the intent of elites with actual effects, confounding analysis of how well presidents succeed compared to their objectives. In addition, the limited research that has been conducted on whether presidents have an effect or not neglects to systematically explore the conditions and selective dimensions of influence.

Research on public opinion and individuals identifies four conditions that modify or obstruct elite efforts to move citizen attitudes. First, when the public holds strong opinions about an issue, it will be difficult to change basic preferences or the importance attached to the policy (Visser, Bizer, and Krosnick 2006; Taber and Lodge 2006; Peffley and Hurwitz 2007). This creates incentives for presidents to use their private polling to focus on weakly held attitudes or gaps in public knowledge. Second, competing messages from other elites and/or the media can neutralize presidential efforts to influence the public's opinions. Research shows that counterframes often offset each other by motivating individuals to resist any one perspective (Druckman 2004). Third, the president's own history sets parameters on what can be done. Presidents with checkered histories on an issue or low credibility may find individuals more inclined to resist or question their messages (Druckman and Lupia 2000; Chong and Druckman 2007). Conversely, public approval of a president's performance increases his influence in moving opinion (Page, Shapiro, and Dempsey 1987; Page and Shapiro 1984; but cf. Cohen 1995). Fourth, efforts by elites to direct public opinion are colored by real-world events, especially if circumstances and communications clash. President George W. Bush's pronouncements about the progress of US forces in Iraq were undercut after 2006 with evidence of a swelling insurgency, much as Lyndon

Johnson's optimism about victory in Vietnam was deflated by the Tet Offensive in 1968 (Ricks 2006; Jacobs and Shapiro 1999).

In short, elite efforts to move voters are not tantamount to effect. Research is needed to assess the effectiveness (or marginal effect) of presidents in changing public opinion in the particular directions they seek. Presidential impact may defy "strong or weak" contrasts in favor of contingencies: presidents may—under certain conditions—nudge policy preferences and prime individuals to elevate the salience of certain topics and to retrieve specific attitudes and beliefs from memory. These effects may fall short of White House (and some scholarly) expectations, but they are also significant tools for agenda setting, organizing how trade-offs are understood, and building support or opposition for certain initiatives.

## Researching Representation

This book investigates the practice of political representation by studying the American presidency and, specifically, three presidents—Richard Nixon, Lyndon Johnson, and Ronald Reagan.

### Enduring Questions

We study presidential strategies to shape public opinion in order to examine three sets of dueling theoretical expectations about political representation. The first set flows from the question, What is represented? Empirical research tends to equate representation with the substantive policy preferences of citizens. In contrast to this "responsiveness account," we consider several plausible alternatives. Substantive representation may be limited to a narrow subset of salient issues. Still further departing from the responsiveness account, presidents may attempt to bypass substantive policy in favor of linkages to voters based on appealing personality traits. Standing for the country through nonpolicy appeals is foreign to most empirical studies of political representation but is familiar to political theorists who have studied the history of representation and its multiple forms (Pitkin 1967).

Chapter 2 begins our investigation into the form of representation that presidents seek by tracing the development of an extensive White House administrative capacity to privately track public opinion and to incorporate polling into White House communications. The locking in of this "public opinion apparatus" (Jacobs 1992a, 1992b, 1993, 2005; Jacobs and Shapiro 1994, 1995b, 1999) across individual presidents demonstrates the institutional presidency's commitment to defining what it represents. Chapter 3 specifically analyzes the political calculations and circumstances that influence why presidents track two distinctive types of information—preferences for specific policies and broad public attitudes toward conservatism and liberalism.

The second set of theoretical expectations concerns the question, Who is represented? The responsiveness account portrays government officials as restricted to following the policy preferences of a majority of the mass public. By contrast, we will demonstrate that presidents (and, specifically, Ronald Reagan) catered to narrow subgroups of Americans—partisan activists, intense and loyal political supporters, and the affluent.

The third set of theoretical expectations concerns how government officials treat citizens. The responsiveness account depicts them as acutely attuned to pleasing their demanding masters in order to minimize the risk of voter punishment for unresponsiveness. In reality, however, presidents routinely attempt to mold the public so that it supports them and their policies. Chapter 5 uncovers White House efforts to prime Americans to focus on selective policy areas in order to affect their evaluations of the president's policies and his public image. Chapter 6 shifts to more explicit White House efforts to change public opinion and, especially, the public's policy preferences. Presidents do exercise selective and conditional influence, but it falls short of their expectations to dominate the public's policy agenda and preferences.

## Research Design and Case Selection

Our investigation of contending accounts of political representation rests on unique evidence and analysis of presidential behavior. Our analysis benefits from previous archival research that traces the origins of an institutionalized public opinion apparatus and the variations and themes in its historical development into the contemporary era. John Geer (1996) builds a general argument for the connection of scientific surveys to American politics, while Robert Eisinger (2003), Dianne Heith (1998, 2003, 2004), and other scholars have cataloged the detailed features of White House polling operations, the particular types of public opinion research assembled by individual presidents and their aides, and the evolution of White House operations to integrate polling results into organizational routines (see Rottinghaus 2010; Murray 2006; and Murray and Howard 2002). The contribution of this research is to reveal the confidential information in the hands of presidents and how it enters into their calculations. This contrasts with the practice of much empirical research inferring motivations from aggregate results or anecdotes—helping explain the portrayal of politicians as skittish antelope (e.g., Erikson, MacKuen, and Stimson 2002).

Although past archival research has amassed rich descriptions of private presidential polling, it has had little impact on broader research and theory relating to political behavior, elite strategizing, and democratic representation. Richly descriptive archival reporting of presidential polling has been disconnected from studies of representation—a loss for both areas of study.

We offer a new approach—one that integrates democratic theory and quantitative analysis with archival research on presidential polling and political strategizing. We draw on theories of institutions and political representation and a mix of research methods to develop and examine falsifiable expectations about the types of public opinion collected and used by presidents, how they segment the public, their specific strategies to move public opinion, and the relative effects of these efforts (King 1993). For the first time, we combine statistical and qualitative methods to rigorously identify how presidents use polls and their effects on presidential behavior and strategy.

Our broad theoretical and analytic approach to private White House polling not only departs from previous presidential research but also challenges past empirical analyses of political representation, which depended on indirect measures of the public's policy preferences from national social science surveys, referenda outcomes, or the presidential vote in a district. Without the actual polling data used by politicians, previous research presumed that publicly available data matched the type of information that politicians actually used. Our unique combination of archival research, quantitative methods, and theory makes it possible both to detect how representation is understood and acted on by actual political elites (and why that is important normatively) and to examine potential gaps between intentions and outcomes—a crucial distinction to avoid overestimating the impact of elites. Chapter 2 supplies in-depth discussion of our data and research methods.

Our book relies on intensive analysis of three presidents—Johnson, Nixon, and Reagan—to address enduring questions about political representation and American politics.[3] These historic cases continue to be instructive with regard to contemporary politics for three reasons. First, archival research and journalist reporting on presidents since Reagan confirm the institutionalization of extensive private polling in the White House's standard operations. There are variations across presidents; Jimmy Carter and George H. W. Bush were personally less interested in polling than Ronald Reagan and Bill Clinton were (Heith 1998, 2003, 2004; Eisinger 2003; Rottinghaus 2010; Murray 2006; Murray and Howard 2002; Jacobs and Shapiro 2000). The enduring nature of White House polling, however, is that it continued despite the relative personal disinterest of the president. Over the past several decades, the particular contexts and features of White House polling have changed, of course: new public opinion tools were tried, the divides between the parties widened, and the nature of presidential appeals to Americans adapted as network media gave way to a plethora of other sources of political information—from cable television to social media. Each of these changes reinforced (or intensified) presidents' motivation to seek opportunities to augment their influence and hone their strategies to move public opinion. We trace these strategies in this book.

Second, our investigations of White House behavior and engagement with broader theories and research of institutions break into the black box of presidential strategizing to reveal, for the first time, the microfoundations of contemporary American politics. For instance, a growing body of empirical research is finding evidence of segmented representation based on aggregate data of income and government policy; this broader body of research guides our analysis of private White House calculations and polling to show their broader theoretical and empirical significance. In comparison to accounts of the presidency as serving the general interest, we trace White House polling and maneuvering to the concrete pressure of organized interests, changing electoral politics, and building of new coalitions. Put simply, our findings often echo broad patterns in previous research—penetrating presidential motivations and strategies in order to raise substantial normative questions about the nature of American political representation.

Third, our research design is tailored to our broader theoretical questions. Although research on presidents typically focuses on intensive description of a small number of administrations (often referred to as the "$N = 1$" challenge), our analysis is geared to increasing the number of observations of presidential decisions and related polling information.

This follows Gary King's (1993) recommendation for "decisionmaking research." More generally, our research design is attuned to a Popperian approach that dominates much of social science research: it accepts the restricted range of settings and the "ambiguity of confirmation" (Cook and Campbell 1979, 21) even as we strive to identify "broad conceptual applicability" (Shadish, Cook, and Campbell 2002, 19). Following Popper, we recognize that hypotheses are never proved; rather, they are tested on available cases and provisionally accepted in the absence of contradictory evidence. This approach is embraced by leading social science scholars such as Shadish, Cook, and Campbell (2002) and is common in American politics research on a single or a few elections, roll call votes, congresspeople, or wars.

## Democratic Theory and the Practice of Political Representation

The framers of the US Constitution designed a democratic republic that rejected acute responsiveness to the demands of the mass public. Instead, they relied on the "scheme of representation" to insulate governing elites and enable them to discern and pursue the public good. One of the ironies of US political history is that what the Constitution's makers sought to avoid—acute responsiveness to the public's opinions—has become the anchor of America's legitimacy. A large and sophisticated body of research in political science and sociology largely confirms the government's responsiveness to general public opinion.

The conventional model of representative democracy bears little resemblance, however, to the realities of elite behavior. This book excavates the actual practice of political representation by presidents. It finds that presidents attempt to circumvent democracy and the authentic views of Americans by shaping the general public's attitudes to mirror theirs, by minimizing (or altogether avoiding) substantive policy responsiveness, and by catering to narrow groups of the politically connected and affluent. These patterns raise profound questions about the nature of representation and democratic theory. We return to these questions in the concluding chapter. We begin by tracing the presidency's focus on public opinion and polling in order to fashion the institutional support that serves the White House's political needs.

### CHAPTER TWO

# The Political Strategy of Tracking the Public

Information is power. Ample and accurate information empowers politicians to pursue their goals—whether they be winning elections or advancing favored policies. For some time, research on American politics emphasized how a lack of information leads politicians to treat voters with timidity to avoid the risk of alienating voters and losing elections. The constraint of imperfect or incomplete information, according to this account, induced a reluctance to pursue bold and divergent policy goals (e.g., Shepsle 1972; Page 1978).

The information that politicians collect, however, receives much less attention, obscuring the determined efforts of authoritative leaders to recast what they represent and to shirk the risk of electoral defeat. As presidential power became anchored in the ability to rally public support, the White House invested enormous time and resources in collecting and using a vast amount of private public opinion surveys to change what Americans believed and to narrow democratic representation.

Crafted communications is, of course, a long-standing art of politics. Modern White House communications stands out for its use of scientific polling to anticipate public reactions *before* presidents speak. Presidents have developed the administrative capacity of a public opinion apparatus to track and use their private polling to calibrate strategy to widen their discretion on government policy while building and retaining public support. They use this institutionalized capacity to precisely fashion their public communications in order to narrow their policy responsiveness to particularly salient issues, cater to politically powerful supporters on other issues that are less salient, and broaden public support through personal appeals.

This chapter spotlights one of the most important and unique features of our study—its investigation of the actual polls collected and used by presidents. The bulk of past research on political representation—the relationship between public opinion and government policy—depended on surveys that were publicly available from media organizations and the academy on the assumption that they mimicked the actual information used by politicians (e.g., Page and Shapiro 1983; Erickson, MacKuen, and Stimson 2002; Soroka and Wlezien 2010). But this approach presumed that information itself drove policy goals when the strategic efforts of politicians may have led them to collect and use different types of information about public opinion. The most direct and reliable way to evaluate the dynamics of representation and the effects of public opinion is to examine the data that presidents themselves collected and used.

Our analyses are the first extensive quantitative and archival research on private presidential polls, and they focus on three administrations—those of Johnson and, especially, Nixon and Reagan. Building on past research (e.g., Eisinger 2003; Heith 2004), we complement the president's private polling data with extensive archival records of often-confidential White House strategy memoranda and interviews with senior administration officials to flesh out administration motivations and intentions instead of imposing outside expectations (as past research has tended to do). Our focus on a small number of presidents poses challenges for generalizability but is unavoidable given the limited access to the archival material of contemporary presidents. A distinguished body of research has, however, generated broader theoretical insights through targeted empirical research on a single or a restricted number of presidents (Edwards 1989, 2007), a single campaign (e.g., Jacobs and Shapiro 1994; Jacoby 1998; Petrocik 1996, 836; Riker 1996), or legislators during a single session (e.g., Bartels 1991). In addition, our quantitative analyses rely on a large number of cases where the presidents possessed public opinion data and made relevant statements, minimizing the liability of studying a single president (King 1993). Finally, our quantitative analyses span parts of three decades, making it possible to identify common, as well as distinctive, patterns.

There are differences across presidents in the degree to which they were personally engaged in private polling or deferred to their White House administrative organizations. Some presidents like Nixon were personally engaged and built the administrative capacity to develop and analyze private polls; others like Reagan largely depended on their administrative capacity (Jacobs and Shapiro 1995b; Eisinger 2003; Heith 2004). While the degree of personal presidential engagement is an intriguing particularistic detail covered in Eisinger (2003) and Heith (2004), our analysis concentrates on the private polls that the White House's administrative structures assembled and, unlike prior work, how the polling results were used. We draw on the institutional approach that is common in the study of the presidency, legislative politics, and economic organizations (e.g., Moe 1993; Pierson 2000; North 1991; Schickler 2001). (When we refer to a president in the coming chapters, we are referring—unless otherwise noted—to the president and his personal staff or, in some cases, to executive branch officials working for the president.)

This chapter examines the origins and development of private presidential polling; these are later analyzed to understand how presidents used them and to what effect. We begin here by broadly outlining the rise of presidential polling as a routine institutional feature of the modern White House. The second section describes the broadly similar types of public opinion information that presidents routinely collect. Third, we discuss the primary activity for which presidents used these data: making public statements. We explain how we measure presidential statements and how we link these statements to the White House's polling data—the foundation of the quantitative analyses we conduct in later chapters.

## The Rise of Presidential Polling

Presidents have long sought to track public opinion (Eisinger 2003; Heith 2004; Rottinghaus 2010). In the nineteenth century and the early twentieth, they relied on informal straw polls, postal correspondence from constituents, and attendance at political rallies and other events to roughly gauge the country's sentiment. Franklin Roosevelt was the first president to receive scientific public opinion surveys, though his access to them was not consistently integrated into routine White House operations (Eisinger 2003).

### The Takeoff

Following Kennedy's election, private presidential polling began in earnest, with Kennedy transferring his campaign polling by Louis Harris into the White House (Jacobs 1992b; Jacobs 1993, chap. 2; Jacobs and Shapiro

1995b). The scope of his polling was limited, however, and it was during the Johnson administration that polling became a fundamental part of White House operations. Indeed, Johnson instructed his aides to track his approval and reelection prospects and pressed them to explain why Americans were reaching their evaluations and how they might be altered.[1] Nixon and his senior advisers were even more intense in equating their political success with "understanding the voters" and using "polling [to] bring out current [public] attitudes on the issues and the candidates." Starting early in his term, Nixon instructed H. R. Haldeman, his chief of staff, to "set up a procedure whereby telephone polls can be taken [to] . . . give us some guidance" as a "permanent concern to the White House" and as means to "get fast checks on specific issues at any time."[2] Reagan continued the developments under Nixon, whose pollsters provided a stable of talent and experience for his Republican successors to draw on.

The swelling of the White House's polling is most plainly evident in the number of its polls. Figure 2.1 shows that Harris provided 15 private surveys to the Kennedy White House, often by relying on ad hoc arrangements such as piggybacking questions on surveys sponsored by other clients. Oliver Quayle, whom Harris had recommended to replace him when he became a public pollster, provided most of the 110 surveys that Lyndon Johnson received. (Johnson temporarily turned to John Kraft and Joseph Napolitan in 1967 and 1968 when he became irritated with Quayle's growing visibility and poll results showing that support for the president was sagging.) Nixon escalated the number of private surveys to 173, relying on a stable of trustworthy pollsters who had Republican bonafides to conduct his research, including established firms such as the Opinion Research Corporation and new upstarts that would become party stalwarts—Robert Teeter's Market Opinion Research and Richard Wirthlin's Decision Making Information. Reagan substantially expanded the number of polls to 204, many of which were conducted by Wirthlin (Jacobs 1992a, 1992b, 1993; Jacobs and Jackson 2004; Jacobs and Shapiro 1995b; Jacobs and Burns 2004).

The growth of presidential polls under Johnson reflected their expansion into a more pervasive influence in the White House, outside election campaigns and emergencies. Even as polling became a more routine feature of White House decision making, most of what was conducted by Johnson, Nixon, and Reagan was geared to preparing for the next presidential election and then subsided as second-term presidents no longer faced reelection.

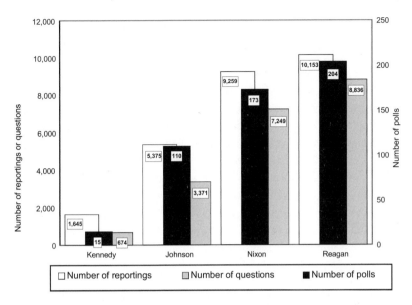

FIGURE 2.1. Scope of Presidential Polling. These counts are of polls that were regularly conducted (with White House input) and forwarded to the president and his top advisers, who
gave them serious attention. Kennedy's principal pollster was Louis Harris, Johnson's was
Oliver Quayle (though Kraft and Napolitan stepped in briefly toward the end of LBJ's term),
Nixon's was Opinion Research Corporation, Chilton, and Market Opinion Research (with
smaller roles by Becker, Behavioral Research, Central, and Decision Making Information),
and Reagan's was Decision Making Information. These counts are from polls conducted after
the president was inaugurated. For more details, see the text. *Source*: Presidential archives.

The White House's polling operations expanded across nearly three decades not only in size but also in specialization. Figure 2.1 shows that the
number of questions asked by presidents increased stepwise from Kennedy to Johnson to Nixon and then to Reagan. We see the same trend as
well with reports to the White House from pollsters on each set of data or
percentages on discrete policies or political issues.

Growing White House specialization in polling is evident in the changing structure of its survey instruments. Kennedy's and Johnson's polls,
which often used the same question format, focused on simple ratings of
job approval, both overall and in terms of salient issues (such as Vietnam),
horse-race pairings with real or possible campaign opponents, and a stable
laundry list of policy issues. By contrast, Nixon and Reagan moved White
House polling from simple, often boilerplate questions that were repeated
for months or years toward more sophisticated and varied surveys based

on relatively sophisticated constructs to advance specific strategic goals. A close reading of the poll questions and reports on survey results under Nixon and Reagan reveals that each administration pursued key trends in public opinion and, perhaps more significantly, designed questionnaires that were rooted in cutting-edge research in the academy and commercial advertising. For instance, Nixon aides and contractors drew on publications in *Public Opinion Quarterly* and recruited graduates of the premier survey research centers such as the University of Michigan's Institute for Social Research.[3] Where Johnson's surveys used an open-ended question to troll for public reactions to the president's personality, Nixon and Reagan used semantic differentials and other constructs to map out interpersonal and performance traits, which then fed into high-level White House discussions of political strategy and plans for shaping public opinion (Druckman, Jacobs, and Ostermeier 2004; Jacobs and Jackson 2004).

Although presidential interest in polling may appear to wax and wane depending on personal taste, White House polling became institutionalized in the office of the presidency as a functionally specialized and organizationally routinized operation (Jacobs 1993; Jacobs and Shapiro 1995b; Ragsdale and Theis 1997). Consistent with the broader patterns of institutional change in the presidency, this public opinion apparatus developed a large specialized staff, professional facilities, and routinized operations to track and use private polling. While Kennedy used ad hoc procedures and stored his polls in his brother's safe in the attorney general's office in order to keep them secret, Johnson established a stand-alone operation overseen by senior aides. He added new staff with responsibility to schedule polls, assemble their results in updated notebooks, analyze them, distribute them to relevant staff, and follow up on Johnson's handwritten requests to "study and talk to [him] about [particular results]."[4] Indicative of how polls were integrated into the administration's organization, more than 90 percent of Johnson's polls during one year were analyzed by a staff member and sent along to a senior staff member, who typically forwarded them to the president.[5]

Nixon's handling of polling paralleled his general hierarchical style of management. His chief of staff personally managed the design and distribution of polls, following up on the president's instructions with orders to his aides. Haldeman's office closely monitored the "drafts of questions and memoranda related to particular poll[s]" to confirm that the vendors were following directions from the president and his senior staff; it also ensured that the timing of polls fit the White House's political needs and updated the "polling books" with the most recent data for use by the president, Haldeman, and other senior administration officials.[6] Typical of Nixon's control over polling, a May 1971 entry in Haldeman's daily diary detailed: "A long review [with the president] of some of the general results of our new image poll that I just received this morning. [The president] had a lot of questions on the specifics and . . . felt that we need to do some additional polling."[7] Numerous White House memoranda and entries in Haldeman's diaries record Nixon's specific instructions about the selection of subject areas, the precise wording of questions, and other detailed features of surveys. In a typical exchange, an aide to Haldeman reported that two White House surveys used "questions [that] have been accumulating for several weeks" and that the "President, you, . . . and other members of the Staff have suggested many of th[e] issue areas for questions."[8] Nearly two years before the 1972 election, Nixon and his senior advisers supervised the construction of the "basic design [of the campaign's] polling effort," insisting that they "review all polls before they are done to make sure that they meet . . . the [campaign's] plan."[9]

Responsibility for polling in the Reagan White House rested with the administration's ruling triumvirate of Edwin Meese, James Baker, and Michael Deaver, who delegated operations to staff and trusted polling specialists. The core of these operations was run by Wirthlin, who conducted monthly surveys and compiled reports of previous research, especially during the height of polling in Reagan's first term.

The integration of polling into the core operations of White House staff (including senior officials) is critical to charting the development of the presidency as an institution and to tracing the attention and influence of public opinion data in White House decisions. Even with variations across administrations, presidents converged over time toward treating private polls as an indispensable and routine instrument for designing strategy and fashioning communications.

*Explaining the Polling Presidency*

The expansion and specialization of presidential polling since Kennedy resulted from a confluence of advances in survey research, changing political motivations, and social learning.

The political crises that sapped the Johnson and then the Nixon presidencies created intense pressure to find means to shore up public and, thereby, political support. Although Johnson and Nixon sported different agendas and staffs, both presidents were intensely motivated to bolster their public support as relations frayed with Congress, key interest groups, and other parts of the Washington establishment (Kernell 1986/2006). They and their staffs latched onto polling as an indispensable tool to track the contours of public opinion for the purpose of designing strategies to sustain support for their distinctive agendas among Americans and Washington insiders.

In addition, the growing influence of core party constituents ratcheted up the political need both to abide by the policy goals of these groups and to find the means to mitigate the electoral risks of defying the general public's policy preferences when that became unavoidable. These shifts in the political system's incentive structure further motivated Nixon and especially Reagan to track the policy preferences of conservatives and other key components of their political base. The political need of the White House to appeal to swing voters (even as it catered to its liberal or conservative base) elevated the strategic attraction of tracking the public's evaluations of the president's personality to pinpoint why Americans liked and disliked him. A careful cataloging of White House polling from Kennedy through Reagan revealed significant increases in the volume of data collected on personal image; Nixon more than doubled his predecessor's magnitude of polling on presidential personality traits, and Reagan expanded Nixon's 55 percent (Jacobs and Burns 2004).

How presidents used polls was informed by what they learned from their predecessors. Nixon's innovations were, in part, propelled by observing Johnson's operation and concluding that there was "power in having the statistics yourself" (as one Nixon aide explained).[10] The Nixon White House also drew on the career experiences of its top staff (including Haldeman) in sophisticated commercial advertising, which drew them to academe and to pollsters such as Teeter and Wirthlin who incorporated the latest survey research advances.[11] The experiences of the Nixon staff with survey research convinced them—as one senior official in the 1972 campaign explained—of its reliability and importance in "provid[ing] a solid basis for strategic and tactical campaign decisions" and guiding the "strategic thrust [of] the campaign."[12]

For Reagan, the learning was direct and personal—his operation borrowed heavily from Nixon's stable of pollsters and extended its inclination to integrate commercial and academic research into political survey research. Reagan also extended Nixon's more adaptive and flexible use of polling. Where Kennedy and Johnson tended to ask about the same set of policy issues, Nixon and then Reagan took a dynamic approach in selecting the domestic and international issues to track. Their administrations added and dropped issues in reaction to new events, public concerns, and anticipation of future administration policy and action. Even as attention to individual issue areas varied, there was a tendency to pay more attention to domestic issues.

The confluence of capacity, motivation, and learning produced an intense and ongoing involvement of the president and senior White House staff in designing questionnaires, analyzing their results, and utilizing the findings.

## The Pillars of Strategic Polling

A large component of American political science is devoted to conducting public opinion surveys and analyzing the patterns and trends in public attitudes thereby revealed. We shift the focus from studying public opinion per se to exploring the extensive information about public attitudes and evaluations that politicians and, specifically presidents, assemble and analyze.[13] Appreciating the vast warehouse of polls that presidents have accumulated is not enough, however. Examining the strategic significance of White House polling leads to a more precise question; what specific *types* of information about public opinion do administrations collect and use?

From the beginning of private White House polling, presidents tracked political "vital signs"—the public's approval of the president's job performance in general (asking, e.g., "Do you disapprove or approve of the job Richard Nixon is doing as president") and the support of voters for the president and other potential candidates in light of upcoming elections. These general vital signs, however, rarely satisfied presidents and their senior staff, who used their private polling to understand why Americans were reaching these overall assessments and how they might be altered. This pushed the White House to expand polling and to specialize its design.

The strategic calculations that drove the overall development of the White House's polling also guided its particular directions. Starting in earnest with Johnson, the White House's political needs drove its collection of data on five categories of public opinion: policy preferences, issue approval, most important problem, personality traits, and subgroup demographics (e.g., social and religious orientations).

*Policy Preferences*

What do voters want? This is an enduring question in electoral politics, and it undergirds much of democratic theory and models of political responsiveness to median voters. It is not surprising, then, that from its beginnings presidential polling tracked the public's policy preferences. What may be surprising, however, is how presidents tracked those preferences.

Specifically, presidents tended to take two distinct approaches to tracking the public's policy views. One approach entailed asking questions about precise attitudes on specific issues. For example, the White House's survey may ask, "Are you in favor or not in favor of cutting federal spending?" or, "Do you believe that spending on national defense should decrease or increase?" or, "Would you favor withdrawal of all US troops from Vietnam by the end of 1971?" Presidents would use these questions to compute the percentage of the public holding a particular view—for example, the percentage who took the conservative positions on a specific issue (e.g., favor cutting federal spending, favor increasing defense spending, oppose troop withdrawal). We call these types of questions *Policy Opinion*.

Of course, administrations recognized that space on survey instruments was limited and that collecting and processing data imposed substantial financial and organizational costs in terms of staff time and attention. These costs, in conjunction with strategic concerns, motivated the White House to also regularly ask about a more generalized measure of policy positions in the form of an *Ideological Identification* item. This question asked respondents to report whether they viewed themselves as liberal or conservative; in many cases, it specifically asked them to place themselves on a scale ranging from very liberal to very conservative. The White House would routinely use those data to identify the percentage of conservative respondents (i.e., the proportion with scores of 5, 6, or 7 would be treated as conservative if the scale ranged from 7 [very conservative] to 1 [very liberal]). In short, the Ideological Identification item was treated as a percentage conservative score. Since Ideological Identification could be queried with a single survey item, it was easy to include on virtually all surveys, and processing costs were minimal. The drawback, of course, is that that single item would fail to pick up subtle variations in liberal and conservative positions on specific issues that could present significant political risks, especially on salient issues.

When presidents relied entirely on Ideological Identification as a way

to track the public's issue preferences, we call it a *lumping* approach—
they essentially were lumping together the public's issue-specific positions
into a single aggregate measure of conservatism/liberalism. When they
depended on issue-specific items, we refer to it as a *splitting* approach.
Tracking particular views on individual issues that defy consistent ideological classification (i.e., the public may adopt liberal positions on some
issues and conservative positions on others) imposed significant costs.
While the White House's strategic calibration of its collection of public
opinion data often followed these distinct approaches, no administration
used the *lumping* and *splitting* monikers.

Why did the White House choose to rely solely on the Ideological
Identification lumping approach or the disaggregated Policy Opinion
splitting items? This choice was not arbitrary. Instead, it was tied to specific political circumstances and White House challenges. Throughout this
book we discuss how presidents made these decisions and how those decisions affected their subsequent behaviors.

*Issue Approval*

Presidents routinely track the public's general evaluation of their job performance. It is one of the most important political vital signs. But it is also
of limited utility in terms of fashioning strategy. Presidents need to know
why their overall approval is low or high in order to lock in support and
counter opposition.

Successive White Houses have developed two methods for tracking the
public's approval of presidential performance on specific issues. First, they
measured the *Public's Approval of the President's Policy Performance*—
that is, they asked survey respondents the extent to which they approved
of the president when it comes to a specific issue (see Petrocik 1996;
Miller and Krosnick 2000). For example, the Nixon administration regularly asked, "Do you approve or disapprove of the way President Nixon is
handling the Vietnam situation?" From this type of measure, the White
House computed the percentage of respondents who viewed the president as doing a good job on the issue. Notice that these questions do not
refer to the president's specific issue position; instead, they focus on his
performance on a specific issue.

Second, presidents gauged the *Public's Support for the President's
Policy Position* on a specific issue. Instead of querying respondents on
whether they approve of how the president is performing on an issue (e.g.,

Vietnam, the economy), these items asked respondents whether they agreed with the president's issue position (e.g., Mendelsohn 1996; Riker 1996; Jacoby 1998). For example, the Nixon White House asked, "Do you support President Nixon in his plan to end the war in Southeast Asia?" The White House similarly used these items to identify the percentage of the public that agreed with the president's position.

As we will discuss in later chapters, data from issue approval survey questions play a vital role in presidential strategies to shape public opinion. Presidents use the data to identify the issues that were most likely to resonate with Americans and influence their evaluations.

### Issue Importance

Not all issues are equal in the eyes of voters. Strategic politicians appreciate that ignoring a hot issue runs the risk of appearing out of touch and that addressing an issue of little interest to voters may squander precious resources. Calibrating what issues to address is essential for presidents given their limited time, the numerous issues they are pressed to confront, and the dueling political pressures they are under to attend to the policy goals of supporters without alienating swing voters on unusually salient issues.

Presidents routinely gauged the issues that the public ranked as nationally important, though there was some variation in how they went about tracking *Issue Importance*. For example, Nixon and Reagan tended to ask respondents to name what they viewed as the single most important problem facing the nation. From this came the percentage of respondents who viewed a given issue as salient. Johnson, in contrast, provided respondents with a list of issues and asked, for each one, whether they viewed it as most important. Despite the specification *most*, nothing prevented respondents from listing multiple issues as most important (and they often did). Regardless, the end result is the percentage of respondents who view an issue as most important or among the most important.

Identifying the issues about which the public most cares equips presidents to signal to voters that they share similar concerns and avoid the risk of appearing out of touch (Hammond and Humes 1995; Traugott and Lavrakas 1996/2000, 31). Polling information on issue importance may also condition how presidents use their data on the public's policy preferences: when the public cares greatly about an issue, the president has an interest in acting as a splitter and attending to detailed policy preferences on that issue rather than the general ideological leanings of the public.

## Beyond Policy Representation: Image

Most research about political representation tends to focus on government policy; for example, do the decisions of elected officials follow the policy preferences of most citizens or politically powerful subgroups? Our research on private White House polls reveals, however, that this presumption is overly narrow. It neglects how presidents use their enormous administrative capacity to attempt to shift the public's evaluations of them from focusing on government policy to concentrating on perceptions of their personality. The strategic commitment to recasting representation from policy to nonpolicy produced significant innovations in Nixon's and Reagan's polling.

Compared to their predecessors, Nixon and Reagan substantially increased polling on the public's perceptions of the president's personality (Jacobs and Burns 2004). Nixon repeatedly pressed his staff on "the job we're to do on the personality side" and insisted on the strategic importance of launching an "overall game plan and presidential offensive project, specifically on the President's image." Even as the White House wrestled with policy issues, its polling and strategizing to shape public opinion also concentrated on "get[ting] across what kind of a man the President is."[14]

The Nixon White House built its private polling operation to track methodically the public's attitudes not only toward government policy but also toward the president's personal image. This included the use of "thermometer ratings": respondents were asked to estimate their general feelings. The most sophisticated and sustained polling on image that the administration collected and used focused on tracking specific personality attributes. The Nixon team drew on cutting-edge survey research to develop a package of questions on paired semantic differentials asking respondents to rate the president along a seven-point scale on a series of opposite adjectives (such as *competent/incompetent* and *strong/weak*).

The Nixon White House's polling team narrowed down the list of semantic differentials to eighteen traits and four general scales: *competence*, *strength*, *warmth*, and *trust*. Each scale consisted of the average public evaluation of the president on the given attribute, with higher scores indicating an increasingly positive perception. The Nixon administration developed these scales on the basis of its reading of scholarly research on personality attributes (e.g., Berlo, Lemert, and Mertz 1969).[15] Its scales tracked two broad (and well-studied) clusters of personality attributes: the *performance-based traits* of competence and strength and the *interpersonal characteristics* of warmth and trust (e.g., Kinder 1986; Iyengar and Kinder 1987, 73–74; Funk 1999, 702). Presidential usage of personality data echoed public opinion research highlighting the primacy of performance-based traits (relative to interpersonal characteristics) (Funk 1999; Iyengar and Kinder 1987; Kinder, Peters, Abelson, and Fiske 1980; Lau 1985; Miller and Krosnick 1996; Miller, Wattenberg, and Malanchuk 1986; Page 1978; Sellers 1998).

The Reagan administration continued to track the public's perceptions of personality. Like the Nixon administration, it measured the four major traits of competence, strength, warmth, and trust. The Reagan team modified Nixon's approach by more often employing questions that directly asked respondents to rate how well a set of traits (e.g., trustworthiness) described the president. From these questions, both administrations computed a *percentage* of respondents who believed the trait described the president well.[16] Reagan also routinely included a basic thermometer measure to gauge on a scale of 0–100 how "well of a person" people perceived him as. White House polling on the public's perceptions of the president's personal traits played a critical role in its strategy. Personality traits fundamentally influenced the issues presidents highlighted in their effort to shape public perceptions.

## *Listening to the Factions: Subgroup Demographics*

Presidents may not follow the policy preferences of the median voters because they are responding to politically vital segments of the electorate. In this way, they may be responsive but still ignore the views of most citizens. For example, they may align their positions with those of wealthy citizens while ignoring the preferences of middle- or lower-income voters (Bartels 2008). When this occurs, they are not pandering to the general public but rather listening to selected parts of the electorate (Wood 2009).

The change in political incentives that elevated the expected returns of catering to party activists and other core supporters motivated presidents to increasingly collect data on subgroups of voters. In particular, the White House asked respondents to self-report various demographic features in order to break up polling data. For example, it differentiated high-income voters' views on welfare spending (e.g., high-income voters may desire decreased spending) from the positions of low-income voters (e.g., low-income voters may favor increased spending). With these data, presidents could selectively respond to groups, ignoring the majority perspective (e.g., keep welfare spending unchanged). Not surprisingly, administrations routinely collected information on the economic attributes of voters—especially income. This echoes research that documents the disproportionate influence of economically advantaged citizens (e.g., Beard 1913; Bartels 2008; Gilens 2005; Jacobs and Page 2005; Bartels 2008; although see Soroka and Wlezien 2008).

Reagan, in particular, sought to broaden subgroup analyses beyond income in order to construct a new conservative coalition. The result is that the Reagan administration carefully tracked the policy preferences of not only high-income earners—often economically conservative or "supply-side" advocates who favored sharp reductions in government taxation—but also social conservatives (especially born-again Protestants and Baptist fundamentalists) and philosophical conservatives. Additionally, it sought to capitalize on the unraveling of the New Deal coalition by tracking the precise opinions of two other political segments that were expected to swing the 1984 elections—the growing ranks of independents who did not identify with the major parties and Catholics who had previously been stalwart Democrats.

## Putting the Polling Data to Work

How do presidents use their extensive and diverse types of information about the attitudes and perceptions of Americans to design strategy? The answer lies not in data alone but rather in the presidential strategy that drove the calibrated collection and use of the White House's private polling. Table 2.1 provides a summary of the central types of public opinion

TABLE 2.1  **Public Opinion Data**

| Variable | Measure | Example(s) |
|---|---|---|
| Policy preferences: | | |
| Policy opinion | Percentage of respondents who take a particular position on an issue (standardized 0–1) | Are you in favor or not in favor of cutting federal spending? |
| Ideological identification | Percentage of respondents who self-identify as conservative (i.e., on the conservative end of the scale) (standardized 0–1 such that 5, 6, 7 indicate conservative, reflecting general pattern in archival records) | Do you think of yourself as closer to being liberal or being conservative? (with response options ranging from extremely liberal to extremely conservative) |

*continues*

TABLE 2.1 (*continued*)

| Variable | Measure | Example(s) |
|---|---|---|
| Issue approval: | | |
| Approval of policy performance | Percentage of respondents who approve of the president's performance on a specific issue (standardized 0–1) | Do you approve or disapprove of the way President Nixon is handling the Vietnam situation? |
| Public support for policy position | Percentage of respondents who agree with the president's position on a specific issue (standardized 0–1) | Do you support President Nixon in his plan to end the war in Southeast Asia? |
| Issue importance | Percentage of respondents who view a particular problem or issue as the most important one facing the country (standardized 0–1) | What would you say is the single most important problem facing the United States today, that is, the one that you, yourself, are most concerned about? |
| Image | Average score of the public's perceptions of the president's competence, strength, warmth, and trustworthiness (focused on positive answered and standardized percentage positive to 0–1 scale) | On the following 7-point scale, rate President Nixon, where 1 = dishonest and 7 = honest. |
| | Percentage of respondents who believe a trait (e.g., trustworthiness) is an excellent or good description of the president (standardized 0–1). | How well do these characteristics [e.g., trustworthy] describe President Reagan? (with response options including excellent, good, only fair, poor, no opinion). |
| | Average rating on a "thermometer scale" (standardized 0–1). | How would you rate Ronald Reagan on a scale from 0 to 100, where the worst possible person . . . would get a rating of 0, while the best possible person would get a rating of 100? |
| Subgroup demographics | Self-reported income, religion, ideology, partisan identification (same as support for policy position but among subgroups only) (standardized 0–1) | Is your religious background Protestant (e.g., Baptist, Methodist, etc.), Roman Catholic, Jewish, or something else? |
| | | Do you consider yourself an evangelical Christian, a fundamentalist, or neither one? |
| | | Which of the following income groups includes your total family income in 1987 before taxes? (with response options including nine distinct income ranges) |

data presidents collected. Coming chapters will be devoted to analyzing how and why presidents used these data.

We use a variety of research tools to understand how the White House used its polling data. Qualitative assessments of memoranda, interviews, and other materials reveal its intentions and internal strategizing. We also use quantitative analyses, as we next discuss, to study the public statements of presidents and how such statements relate to aggregated monthly polling measures.

## Studying Presidential Statements

Unlike legislators, who cast public votes in committees and on the House or Senate floor, presidents generally make decisions behind closed doors. But they do enjoy unrivaled opportunities to talk to millions of Americans directly through nationally televised speeches in prime time and indirectly through the coverage of the media, which follows them around the clock. They use this extraordinary access to the public for specific strategic purposes—to reveal policy decisions reached behind closed doors, to deploy carefully crafted words and arguments to raise the salience of an already announced policy or persuade Americans to support it, and to profile a dimension of their personality to strengthen their appeal (Cohen 1995; Kernell 1986/2006; Jacobs and Shapiro 2000; Riker 1996). We analyze how and under what conditions the White House's private polls convince the president to tailor his public statements to pursue one of these strategies.

Indicative of the political importance the White House attaches to fashioning the president's public statements, Johnson and his team seized on the presidency's "capacity to change the public mood" to "make a massive and concerted effort to create a more positive, constructive, affirmative mood." The president's public statements and his office's unique visibility were expected to capture and "maintain press concentration on the White House as the vital center of news and interpretation."[17] Nixon's advisers were a bit more nuanced, strategically calibrating the emphasis and space that the president allocated to particular issues as a tool that they expected to "create issues" and "focus" public attention. The White House's detailed attention to the issues Nixon singled out and how he addressed them followed from his demand for a "totally oriented commitment to relating everything we do to the political side" and for his aides to be constantly asking, "Does this help us politically?"[18]

We analyze presidential strategy by measuring its most directly available indicator—presidents' public statements. In particular, we conducted a rigorous content analysis of Johnson's, Nixon's, and Reagan's statements on the full range of domestic and foreign policy issues in all news

collection and analysis. This institutional development of the presidency reflects changes in the broader environment of American politics that motivated presidents to widen their leeway to cater to the most intense and valued supporters while continuing to appeal to swing voters necessary to secure reelection for themselves and their allies.

Presidents tailored the specific content and scope of their survey research to serve their strategic needs by selectively responding to segments of the electorate and by attempting to persuade Americans to change their policy preferences or alter their evaluations of presidents by focusing on personality traits instead of substantive policy. How the strategic needs of presidents factor into their collection and use of distinct types of polling data is the topic to which we next turn. We will show that presidential use of public opinion differs in dramatic ways from the conventional way in which scholars construe and study responsiveness.

PART II

# Presidential Strategies to Shape Public Opinion

### CHAPTER THREE

# How White House Strategy Drives the Collection and Use of Its Polling

Presidents hunger for information about public opinion to enhance communication that will advance their political interests and improve their ability to move public attitudes. Despite its massive capacity for polling, the White House faces limits on how much and what kinds of polling data it can collect. Survey instruments have space constraints, and the collection and processing of data come with substantial financial and organizational costs. These constraints—combined with the intense political interests of presidents—pressure them to make choices and act as strategic gatherers of information rather than relying on arbitrarily assembled data.

Which public opinion data are most valuable to politicians? Previous research has not rigorously investigated why politicians decide to *collect* and *use* and which type is most strategically attractive (cf. Burstein 2003; Wlezien 2004).

Presidents tailor the information they collect and use to critical political circumstances—the proximity to Election Day, the coherence and salience of public attitudes toward specific problems or issues, changing political party dynamics, and the particular demands of domestic and foreign policy. The mix of challenges facing presidents shapes the distinctive contours of how they approach information gathering.

Its strategy regarding information shaped how the White House handled two of the most politically important types of polling data. The first type is the public's Ideological Identification—its aggregating of policy attitudes into one global measure of general ideological predisposition, which we refer to as *lumping*. The second type is the public's Policy Opinions—its disaggregated preferences for specific policies, which we refer to as *splitting*. In policy domains and electoral situations that politically threaten presidents, the White House is motivated to invest time in finding information on specific issues that the public ranks as important or salient; absent public scrutiny and the risk of damaging punishment during an approaching election, it is motivated to rely on less costly information related to general ideological orientation.

In this chapter, we explore the distinctive approaches to lumping and splitting by Nixon and Reagan as they set about crafting their public presentations. Reagan invested most extensively in collecting and using data on both ideological orientations and policy preferences in order to stake out conservative positions that appealed to party activists and his strongest supporters while ducking land mines for swing voters. Nixon was less inclined to aggressively push a conservative agenda, preferring instead to hug the main contours of public opinion and selectively seize on opportunities to move to the right as conditions allowed.

We begin by exploring research on political representation to sketch potential political motivations for lumping and splitting and then proceed to analyze how and under what political and policy conditions Nixon and Reagan modulated their approach to information.

## Lumping versus Splitting

Research on political representation has largely neglected how government officials track and use public opinion but nonetheless offers insights into the motivations that might affect how politicians approach information. Research by Erikson, MacKuen, and Stimson (2002, xxi, 289–91) indicates that "political leaders regularly ignore expressed public preferences on [specific policies] . . . knowing that the preferences arise from a weak grasp of the central facts." Instead, "it is the general public disposition, the mood, which policy makers must monitor." Kingdon (1984, 68–69, 153) similarly concludes that government officials rely on "general judgments about the state of public opinion," such as the sense of an "antigovernment mood in the country." This research suggests that politicians have incentives to act as lumpers who discount the public's specific policy preferences if they conclude that the public lacks the necessary information and attention to form specific views on individual policies and accurately scrutinize its specific positions. Under these conditions, politicians may focus on the electorate's mood—the coherent, homogenous direction that underlies all its considerations and views of apparently dissimilar policies.

In contrast to lumping, splitting is based on the assumption that the public's preferences for specific policies are—under certain circumstances—meaningful and likely to produce potentially damaging scrutiny of politician's public positions. Under these conditions, investing resources in private polling to follow the public's policy preferences is worthwhile to strategic politicians (Monroe 1979, 1998; Page and Shapiro 1983; Geer 1991, 1996; Heith 1998, 2003; Manza and Cook 2002a, 2002b; Page 2002; Eisinger 2003; Wlezien 2004; Soroka and Wlezien 2005).

In addition to factoring in its appraisal of public opinion, the White House's collection and use of lumping or splitting data are also affected by its strategic circumstances and its perception of voter scrutiny and punishment. Politicians are motivated to invest resources in splitting on issues when they perceive risk in the face of an upcoming election (e.g., G. C. Wright 1989; Jacobs and Shapiro 2000; Canes-Wrone 2006; but cf. Rottinghaus 2010), the public's perception of particular policies as salient (Page and Shapiro 1983), the emergence of what are seen as intractable or threatening issues in foreign or domestic policy (Nincic 1990; Fiorina 1981; Kahneman and Tversky 1984), or the intensification of political party competition (Aldrich 1995; Carmines and Stimson 1989). This is consistent with previous research demonstrating that salient policies tend to generate greater government responsiveness to majority public opinion on those specific issues (Kuklinski and Elling 1977; Kuklinski and McCrone 1980; Page and Shapiro 1983; Wlezien 2004; Hill and Hurley 1999) and contribute to public attitudes that are more coherent and engaged in forming evaluations of candidates (Krosnick 1988, 1989, 1990; Iyengar 1990).

Absent the risk of unusual public scrutiny, politicians have incentives to rely on less costly information gleaned from Americans' general ideological orientation. In particular, lumping is a reasonable strategy when elections are not imminent and when issues and policy domains are less important to the public and do not involve intractable foreign or domestic challenges that are the subject of intense party competition. Under these conditions, the public's attitudes are typically less reliable, stable, and coherent (Zaller 1992; Druckman and Lupia 2000) and, as a result, pose a less direct threat to politicians.

The confluence of White House assessments of the public's relative attentiveness and knowledge and the risk of voter scrutiny and punishment suggests four general scenarios. The first two are when circumstances point the White House in one consistent direction toward either "Pure Splitting" (it perceives clear risks and demands information on the public's specific policy preferences) or "Pure Lumping" (it senses minimal political threats and is content to track the public's general conservative or liberal tilt). The third scenario is geared toward "Strategic Balancing" by engaging in both splitting and lumping to reduce risks while avoiding massive investments. The fourth scenario is for situations where presidents forgo opinion data of any sort owing to the certainty of their position or constraints on White House polling.

## Lumping and Splitting Data

We examine the general question of whether, why, and how politicians collect and use different types of information on public opinion by studying the content of the survey research conducted by the Nixon and Reagan presidencies and their approaches to incorporating that research in their political strategies. In particular, we investigate the conditions under which the Nixon and Reagan White Houses engaged in lumping (i.e., focusing on the Ideological Identification measure) or splitting (i.e., focusing on Policy Opinion measures) by identifying the statistical associations between private polling data and presidential statements. More precisely, we pinpoint the relative effects of the two polling measures under different political conditions. Policy Opinion, as we explained in the previous chapter, reports the percentage of respondents taking a conservative position on specific issues—such as the percentage taking the conservative position in response to the question, "Are you in favor or not in favor of cutting federal spending?" For the regression analysis, we standardize finite percentage scales or position scales to range from 0 to 1; in the descriptive tables of our data, we leave the numbers at their full scales to provide a better grasp of the actual percentages. (We adopt this as a general practice throughout the book.)

Collection of these types of data provides a measure of White House attention to splitting. Ideological Identification, in contrast, reports the percentage of the public that self-identifies as generally conservative.[1] The gathering of these data serves as an appropriate indicator of lumping even though the White House's construct differs from some previous work on lumping, such as Stimson's (1991) "public mood" measure. (We substituted Stimson's public mood measure in our analyses below and found quite similar results [for more details, see Druckman and Jacobs 2006].)

To detect White House decisions, we tracked presidential statements. We coded our Presidential Policy Positions measure on a five-point scale with higher scores indicating an increasingly conservative position. This allowed us to examine whether the statement data scale moves in congruent directions with the public opinion data scale.[2] The lumping and splitting scenarios each predict a significant and positive relationship between the direction of the president's statements and his Ideological Identification and Policy Opinion data, respectively.

We created the data set by merging the presidential statement data with the public opinion data so that we have a potential observation for each issue during each month for Nixon and Reagan (as explained in chapter 2). The data set also includes public opinion data on issue importance as that may condition lumping and splitting. Both Nixon and Reagan tracked issue importance by asking respondents to state the single most important problem facing the country—this measure reports the percentage who name a given issue.

Because the Nixon data covered forty-nine issues over forty-seven months, there is a potential for 2,303 observations for Nixon (assuming that he made a statement on every issue in each month [49 × 47]). The Reagan data spanned ninety-eight issues over ninety-seven months, leading to 9,506 potential observations. In practice, however, the presidents did not make a statement on every issue in every month. Nixon made a total of 1,288 statements on different policies in the given months; each of these 1,288 statements (or observations) represents the aggregated measures for each policy that he addressed during a given month (such as the conservative direction of all his statements on controlling inflation in January 1972 or fighting crime in February 1972). Reagan made a total of 3,261 statements on different policies in the given months.

In addition, neither president (especially Reagan) collected public opinion data on every issue over time; we analyzed the relationship between statements and public opinion data only when the public opinion data existed.[3] The result is that the effective number of cases for each president was often substantially reduced, as we report below.

Presidents collected and used their private polling data over time. As such, we study this dimension of our data in two ways. First, we use lagged versions of both Ideological Identification and Policy Opinion data (and issue importance) to reflect the White House's operations and decision-making process. This lag captures the time it took for the survey organizations to enter and analyze their results and for the White House to weigh the results and incorporate them into presidential activities. White House records and other evidence (such as memoirs and diaries) suggest that presidents were quite attentive to creating and updating "poll books" that allowed them to regularly consult previous results—even if this meant going back in time. Accordingly, our lagged variables used the most recent data completed at least one month earlier.[4] For instance, we related Nixon's policy statements (i.e., our variable Presidential Policy Positions) in April 1972 to his polling data in March 1972 or, if data were not collected in March 1972, then to the polling data from the previous month for which they were available (whether February 1972, January 1972, or still further back).

Second, we include a lagged value of our dependent variable, Presidential Policy Positions. We expect a strong positive relationship between prior and present Presidential Policy Positions given the incremental nature of policy movement (Wildavsky 1964; Erikson, MacKuen, and Stimson 2002, 285). This provides a tough test of our models: including the lagged dependent variable serves as a control for various other influences that may have affected the prior position of presidents (e.g., interest group activities).

We integrate these quantitative analyses with archival research to explore the White House's intentions and strategies. This anchors our assumptions and interpretations in the actual internal deliberations within the Nixon and Reagan administrations.

Throughout the book, our hypotheses are directional, and our quantitative analyses employ one-tailed tests, following Blalock's (1979, 163) classic advice. This is consistent with White House memos that focused more on general substantive trends than on specific statistical cutoffs.

## Strategic Investments in Information

We begin by examining four scenarios accounting for how the Nixon and Reagan teams engaged in lumping or splitting before public statements:

- Independence when the president had no opinion data of any sort
- Pure Splitting when the president had only Policy Opinion data

- Pure Lumping when the president had only Ideological Identification data
- Strategic Balancing when the president had both types of data

Table 3.1 reports the percentage and number of statements for each of these four scenarios. The rows identify statements for which a president had general data on Ideological Identification (or not), while the columns capture availability of the policy-specific Public Opinion data. (To be considered available, the data must have been collected by the White House at least one month prior to a statement.)

Indicative of the new era of presidents' investment in polling to fashion their public communications, Nixon and Reagan rarely spoke publicly without information on public opinion. Table 3.1 reveals that independence from public opinion data declined from 19 percent under Nixon (223 statements out of a total of 1,180) to zero under Reagan. In other words, Reagan made no statements without public opinion data on either the public's general ideological orientations or its specific policy preferences.

Although both presidents hungered for extensive polling that balanced its costs and benefits, they pursued distinctive strategic aims. Reagan aggressively sought out conservative positions while ducking land mines for

TABLE 3.1  **Availability of Data on Policy Preferences and Ideological Orientation When Nixon and Reagan Made a Statement**

|  | Policy Opinion Data Not Available | | Policy Opinion Data Available | | Total | |
|---|---|---|---|---|---|---|
|  | Nixon | Reagan | Nixon | Reagan | Nixon | Reagan |
|  | Independent | | Pure Splitting | | | |
| Ideological identification data not available | 19 | 0 | 5 | 0 | 24 | 0 |
|  | (223) | (0) | (54) | (0) | (277) | (0) |
|  | Pure Lumping | | Strategic Balancing | | | |
| Ideological identification data available | 39 | 18 | 37 | 82 | 76 | 100 |
|  | (462) | (459) | (441) | (2,057) | (903) | (2,516) |
| Total | 58 | 18 | 42 | 82 | 100 | 100 |
|  | (685) | (459) | (495) | (2,057) | (1,180) | (2,516) |

*Note*: Each cell reports the percentage (and absolute number) of statements for which Nixon or Reagan had a given type of data at least one month earlier.

swing voters, while Nixon was more hesitant about pursuing a conservative agenda.

Given their low costs, it is unsurprising that data on the public's general ideology (Ideological Identification) were extensively collected by both presidents. Table 3.1 shows that Nixon had data on Ideological Identification for 76 percent, or 903, of his statements and that Reagan possessed it for all his statements. Both administrations collected data on the public's ideological orientations substantially more often than they did on the public's policy-specific preferences (Policy Opinions). This is in keeping with the White House's strategic allocation of resources: the low cost and simplicity of tracking the public's ideology made it a good investment for developing a readily available stream of information for crafting presidential statements.

The two Republican presidents did differ, however, on the extent to which they relied on a lumping strategy. Nixon most often pursued a pure lumping approach: he possessed *only* aggregated data on Ideological Identification for 39 percent of the president's public positions, while Reagan was half as likely to collect *only* aggregate information (i.e., for 18 percent of public positions). The strategic significance of this balance is revealing; as we discuss below, Reagan collected a broader scope of information in order to identify opportunities to move in conservative directions.

The higher cost and complexity of collecting polling data on specific policies create disincentives for the White House to invest in them. Nixon depended on polling data alone for only 5 percent of his statements, and Reagan never relied only on Policy Opinion results (he always had data on Ideological Identification).

Reflecting its efforts to expand the Republican coalition while holding on to swing voters, the Reagan White House invested far more heavily in collecting the maximum amount of information than did the Nixon administration. Reagan possessed data on both ideology and specific policies for 82 percent of his statements, as compared to Nixon's 37 percent. Pursuing the strategic balancing strategy allowed both presidents (and, especially, Reagan) to minimize their political risks.

## The Differential Impacts of White House Polling Information

The selective *investment* in different types of public opinion does not explain the relative *impact* of distinctive types of polling information. We examine two of the information scenarios based on the tendency of the Nixon and Reagan White Houses to use only aggregated data about the public's ideology or data on both ideology and specific policies:[5]

1. *The pure lumping scenario.* Before Nixon or Reagan makes a policy statement, the White House possesses *only* Ideological Identification data.
2. *The strategic balancing scenario.* Nixon or Reagan makes a policy statement with both Policy Opinion and Ideological Identification data on hand.

For each of these two feasible scenarios, we regress our Presidential Policy Positions variable (i.e., statements by Nixon and Reagan) on the public opinion data that the White House possessed in one of the scenarios. We scale the public opinion data—both Ideological Identification and Policy Opinions—on 0–1 scales (with 1 representing the strongest conservative position).

In situations where both presidents pursued the pure lumping strategy, Reagan was much more sensitive than Nixon was to data reporting a shift in a more conservative direction.[6] Table 3.2 (cols. 1–3) shows that the public's (conservative) ideology had significant effects for Reagan but not for Nixon (col. 3 vs. col. 2).[7] When Reagan possessed only data on Ideological Identification, he moved his statements toward greater conservatism ($p \leq .05$). We suggest below that this attentiveness to ideology is not uniform but rather strategically calibrated to balance the risk of alienating median voters against the pursuit of economic and social conservatives. Not surprisingly, Reagan and Nixon tended to stick with a position once they stated it publicly, as indicated by the statistical significance of the lagged dependent variable for this and other regressions.

We assess the substantive impact of Ideological Identification by looking at the change in Reagan's position when the public moved from 5 percent below the average conservativeness to 5 percent above its mean (i.e., the public becomes in total 10 percent more conservative). When these changes in public opinion occurred, Reagan moved his position on average in a conservative direction by 19 percent.[8] This is an impressive, statistically significant effect: *White House poll reports of greater conservatism freed Reagan to adopt more conservative positions above and beyond what might be expected on the basis of other forces.* (The inclusion of the lagged dependent variable allows us to control for his prior position and all the factors that went into determining his prior position.)

When Reagan invested in collecting data on the public's specific preferences, however, he resisted a full-bore ideological strategy; he favored the

TABLE 3.2 **Impact of Public Opinion Data on the Domestic and Foreign Policy Positions of Nixon and Reagan (Base Model; Dependent Variable: Presidential Policy Positions)**

| | Presidential Use of Public Opinion Information | | | | | |
| --- | --- | --- | --- | --- | --- | --- |
| | Only Lumping | | | Strategic Balancing | | |
| | (1) Both Presidents | (2) Nixon | (3) Reagan | (4) Both Presidents | (5) Nixon | (6) Reagan |
| Ideological identification | .43** | .13 | 1.93** | −.06 | −.16 | .30* |
| | (.14) | (.13) | (.55) | (.12) | (.13) | (.22) |
| Policy opinions | ... | ... | ... | .16** | .16** | .16** |
| | | | | (.03) | (.05) | (.03) |
| Presidential policy | .78** | .79** | .67** | .78** | .82** | .77** |
| positions, $t-1$ | (.02) | (.03) | (.04) | (.01) | (.03) | (.01) |
| Constant | −.15* | −.02 | −.93** | .08 | .10 | −.12 |
| | (.08) | (.07) | (.33) | (.07) | (.08) | (.13) |
| $R^2$ | .63 | .64 | .48 | .66 | .73 | .64 |
| $N$ | 883 | 460 | 423 | 2,495 | 440 | 2,055 |

*Note*: The table reports OLS coefficients with standard errors in parentheses. ** $p \leq .05$, * $p \leq .10$, one-tailed test.

splitter strategy adopted by Nixon in order to carefully stake out public positions on particular policies. In particular, Nixon's and Reagan's public statements were influenced by White House polling on specific policies in cases where they possessed both Ideological Identification and Policy Opinion data (see table 3.2, cols. 4–6, where the coefficients are in fact identical—the impact is consistent). As more of the public became conservative on *specific* policies, so did both presidents ($p \leq .05$). Although costly, the White House's collection of fuller information prompted Reagan (along with Nixon) to avoid a lumping strategy: Ideological Identification is incorrectly signed in a negative direction for Nixon and only marginally significant for Reagan (cols. 5–6).

In sum, when White House polling was restricted to tracking Ideological Identification, these data had statistically significant effects on Reagan's statements. When the White House was able to invest in collecting both aggregated and disaggregated data, however, polling information on specific policies produced statistically significant effects, and these impacts were evident for both Nixon and Reagan.[9] *Fuller information matters, and presidents capitalize on their costly investment in collecting detailed information on the public's detailed policy views.*

These analyses assume, however, that presidents treat information in similar ways regardless of their political situation (as indicated by their placement in the electoral cycle) or whether they're dealing with domestic or foreign policy. We now consider the conditionality of information, beginning by examining policy domain effects.

## The Conditioning Effects of Policy Domain

In keeping with their distinctive political strategies, Reagan was more inclined than Nixon to adopt conservative positions across domestic and foreign policy domains when polling was restricted to tracking general ideology. Table 3.3 (cols. 1–2) shows that possessing polling data only on ideology prompted Nixon to become more conservative on domestic policy statements ($p \leq .10$) but had no effect on his foreign policy pronouncements.

By contrast, Reagan's statements on *both* domestic and foreign policy were influenced by ideological orientation and at a higher level of statistical significance ($p \leq .05$) (table 3.3, cols. 3–4). If the public moves 5 percent over the average conservatism score, Reagan becomes about 30 percent more conservative in his statements on domestic policy (as compared to just under 2 percent for Nixon under analogous circumstances) and about

TABLE 3.3 **Impact of Public Opinion Data on the Domestic (Dom.) or Foreign (For.) Policy Positions of Nixon and Reagan (Domain Effect Model; Dependent Variable: Presidential Policy Positions)**

| | Presidential Use of Public Opinion Information | | | | | | | |
|---|---|---|---|---|---|---|---|---|
| | Only Lumping | | | | Strategic Balancing | | | |
| | Nixon | | Reagan | | Nixon | | Reagan | |
| | (1) Dom. | (2) For. | (3) Dom. | (4) For. | (5) Dom. | (6) For. | (7) Dom. | (8) For. |
| Ideological | .21* | .01 | 2.91** | 1.27** | −.06 | −.14 | −.02 | .85** |
| identification | (.15) | (.23) | (1.03) | (.60) | (.18) | (.14) | (.27) | (.39) |
| Policy | ... | ... | ... | ... | .53** | −.01 | .28** | −.04 |
| opinions | | | | | (.10) | (.05) | (.05) | (.05) |
| Presidential | .82** | .75** | .55** | .77** | .60** | .93** | .73** | .76** |
| policy | (.03) | (.05) | (.06) | (.04) | (.05) | (.03) | (.02) | (.02) |
| positions, | | | | | | | | |
| $t − 1$ | | | | | | | | |
| Constant | −.07 | .06 | −1.42** | −.60* | −.02 | .11 | .04 | −.34 |
| | (.09) | (.13) | (.62) | (.36) | (.12) | (.09) | (.16) | (.23) |
| $R^2$ | .68 | .58 | .33 | .60 | .65 | .87 | .68 | .58 |
| $N$ | 296 | 164 | 167 | 256 | 255 | 185 | 1,339 | 716 |

*Note*: The table reports OLS coefficients with standard errors in parentheses. ** $p \leq .05$, * $p \leq .10$, one-tailed test.

13 percent more conservative on foreign policy. His conservative disposition across policy domains is consistent with the results shown in table 3.2 above for the lumping scenario.

When Nixon and Reagan possessed polling data on ideology and policy, they both engaged in strategic balancing by tailoring their statements on domestic and foreign policy to accord with their political circumstances, though Reagan continued to be more attuned to general conservatism. Echoing a persistent pattern, table 3.3 indicates that White House data on general ideological orientation influenced Reagan's foreign policy comments ($p \leq .05$) (col. 6 vs. col. 8)). By comparison, White House polling on the public's specific policy preferences had no statistically significant effects on Nixon's or Reagan's foreign policy statements but did influence the domestic positions of both Nixon ($p \leq .05$) and Reagan ($p \leq .05$).

Differences across policy domains in how the White House collected and used its polling data reflect distinct political configurations. *When Reagan was operating with ample information, he relied on general ideological data to appeal to conservatives in his base on foreign affairs and, in particular, on the Cold War. Conversely, he turned his attention to the administration's polling on specific policies to tailor his public positions on domestic issues that are often more consequential for centrist voters. Nixon, by comparison, was more cautious; he found the most salient foreign policy issue of his time—Vietnam—too polarizing to bend to conservatives.*

### The Conditioning Effects of the Election Cycle

The election cycle also conditions how presidents use their polling information. During his second term, when he no longer faced reelection, Reagan was not responsive to either Ideological Identification or Policy Opinion information in the area of foreign policy. This suggests that reelection and his drive to placate his conservative base spurred him to fashion his public positions on foreign affairs, as detected in the results reported in table 3.3. After he won a second term, the influence of party activists on his lame-duck term waned, a fact that interacted with important changes in the prevailing reality—most notably, the thaw in US-Soviet relations and the coming collapse of the Soviet Union.

In short, Nixon and Reagan possessed similar polling capacities and even similar polling expertise, but the particular political and policy circumstances they faced prodded them to differentiate how they used the distinct types of information at their disposal. Reagan was more geared than Nixon toward appealing to general ideological conservatism. In addition to possibly reflecting variations in temperament and philosophies, the differences in how Nixon and Reagan relied on polling information may also stem from changes in the political parties and, especially, the growing influence of conservative party activists within the Republican Party after the late 1970s (Aldrich 1995; Jacobs and Shapiro 2000). Moreover, policy domains also conditioned the use of different types of polling information: electoral risks and rewards are more intense and direct in domestic than in foreign affairs, increasing the political incentives to closely monitor public opinion in general and to give careful consideration to the public's specific policy preference in particular. Finally, electoral cycles influenced Reagan's pursuit of foreign policy, leading to a less ideological approach after his reelection and greater independence from his polling data.

## Presidential Motivations for Collecting Policy Opinion Data

We have seen that presidents vary in how they use polling information given the types of data available, the policy domain, and the timing during the election cycle. A basic question remains, however: *Why* do politicians choose to make substantial investments in collecting polling data and particular types of data?

The substantial rise of presidential polling after World War II coincides with the unraveling of the New Deal coalition and a search for new means to reliably track voters. At the same time, presidents and other political leaders were less confident in long-standing gauges of public opinion—from Congress and political parties to interest groups (Eisinger 2003; Geer 1996).

In addition to adapting to general pressures, Nixon and Reagan faced distinct political incentives in deciding when to collect costly data on specific policy issues. For Nixon, the key factor was the public's ranking of particular issues as important. When voters saw an issue as important, Nixon was apt to collect Policy Opinion data on that issue. Indeed, on issues for which he collected Policy Opinion data, the average importance score, one month prior to data collection, was more than threefold higher.[10]

By comparison, the ranking of an issue's importance had no significant effect on Reagan's decisions on the content of his polls and the collection of Policy Opinion.[11] While the amount of issue-specific data Nixon collected is highly correlated with the average importance of an issue $r = .62, p < .01$), there was virtually no relationship for Reagan (insignificant correlation of .01).

While Reagan's investment in Policy Opinion was not driven by salience, it was informed by his dual political strategy of sustaining his appeal to swing voters even as he aggressively pursued conservative policy goals. His public statements were a third more conservative than Nixon's.[12] These right-wing positions left Reagan exposed to potential backlash by median voters and help account for his investment in tracking the public's specific policy preferences. He collected twice as much Policy Opinion data when making a statement as did Nixon (82 vs. 42 percent; see table 3.1 above). This equipped him to anticipate broader public reactions before staking out a conservative ideological position.

Reagan's collection of Policy Opinion to calibrate his dual strategy of moving right while holding the center not only influenced his positions but also appears to have affected how he communicated. Reagan was twice as likely to make a public statement about a specific policy when he had polling data on it as opposed to when he lacked information on it; Nixon was equally prone to make a statement regardless of whether or not he possessed Policy Opinion data.[13] This pattern holds up across policy domains and when issues are ranked as important.[14]

Reagan collected Policy Opinion data for the strategic purpose of anticipating the impact of his publicly stated positions. This helped minimize the risk of alienating median voters even as he catered to economic and social conservatives. In contrast to Nixon, he was not influenced by the electoral motivations of responding to specific issues that the public ranked as important. Policy goals dominated his administration, and he turned to polls as a kind of early warning system to identify potential risks in talking about issues that were important to him and his allies and that he wanted to explain publicly. In short, the confluence of electoral and policy goals along with the differing costs of polling on ideology and specific policies explains Nixon's and Reagan's particular approaches to publicly stated positions.

## Strategizing within the White House

Quantitative findings mesh with the White House's internal strategizing. For Nixon, the statistical analyses reflect the sustained effort of the president and senior officials to lock in the support of their conservative political base while simultaneously appealing to swing voters. Empirical evidence suggesting that Nixon responded to ideology on less important issues meshes with the advice of his aides to seize opportunities to appeal to his conservative "natural base" in order to dampen "right wing Republican unhappiness because we're not adequately cutting spending, welfare, etc. and they feel we're softening in Vietnam."[15] Nixon was alarmed by criticism from prominent conservatives like Kevin Phillips and Pat Buchanan (who served in the White House) that "we basically had sold out all of our Republican conservative policies in our 'move to the left.'" Moreover, the diary of H. R. Haldeman records numerous meetings in which the president insisted that "we need the group enthusiasm of the right wing" and had to "maintain the conservative support." The administration, he demanded, had to "quit zigzagging and establish a cutting edge" in a "clear-cut," "tougher," "very hard direction" that "establish[es] an awareness of our philosophy to get the government cut down." He insisted: "There's no mileage politically for a conservative Administration in pushing how much we're spending, because the opposition will always spend more. . . . We can't gain on the liberals, but we can sure cool off the conservatives."[16]

Archival records suggest that Nixon and his advisers collected and used their private polls on Ideological Identification to pinpoint where the public shared the conservatism of Nixon's political base. Nixon became convinced that, "based on polls, there are twice as many conservatives as Republicans."[17] Haldeman's staff and other advisers believed that "the American people tend to categorize themselves as conservative more than as liberal."[18] A study of Virginia in January 1972 paralleled the findings of a number of other state surveys: "voters' ratings of the candidates and themselves on the liberal-conservative continuum" showed that "Nixon is closest to the voters in terms of political ideology."[19] On less salient issues, it appears that Nixon and his aides believed that conservative policy positions were critical to holding their political base.

Nixon and his senior advisers, however, accepted that centrist "split-ticket" voters were as important as the conservative base because they would provide the margin of victory. The president's team calculated that they could win over these voters by using his position on salient and popular issues.

Internal archival records reinforce our statistical results showing the White House's predisposition to track the public's policy preference on salient issues and to use that information in designing Nixon's statements; aides relied on their "polls on issues" to address the concern of "whether our position [on specific issues] has gone up or down in the eyes of the public."[20] Nixon and his senior advisers were attuned to polling information on specific issues of *"particular importance to independent and swing voters."*[21] Teeter ran multivariate models for the general electorate to support his argument that "ideology exerted little influence" on vote choice.[22] Even as Nixon was pressured by his base, he and his advisers accepted that reelection depended on "monopolizing the center" and not "go[ing] all conservative."[23] John Ehrlichman, the senior White House official in charge of domestic policy, counseled Nixon against "the pure conservative line which Phillips peddles" in favor of a "domestic course that is down the center" on policy issues.[24]

Reagan's catering to the GOP political base as compared to swing voters contrasts with Nixon's strategy. Archival records of internal White House planning mesh with our earlier findings that Reagan aggressively pursued a strategy to advance the conservative policy goals that he and his allies embraced.

Reagan's fidelity to conservative policy goals was vividly displayed in the opening months of his administration when he knowingly contradicted the public's policy preferences as preparations were made for the inauguration and its initial proposals to set priorities and the public's impressions of the new president. At this critical opening juncture, Reagan's pollster (Richard Wirthlin) conducted extensive national polling to "test" the relationship between the public's policy preferences and Reagan's policy goal of "limit[ing] . . . government spending." Wirthlin urgently reported major public opposition to the president's proposals for cutting Social Security benefits. He dutifully reported to the White House's senior leadership in May 1981 that the president's Social Security proposals had precipitated a threatening tag team—they were very salient and the president's "most unpopular position taken to date." Reagan's Social Security proposal, Wirthlin warned, was "the most potentially damaging issue we face" as it had quickly produced a "significant fall in the number of people who believe that [Reagan] cares about the needs of the elderly and poor" and a "rising feeling that the 49 billion dollar budget cuts will inevitably hurt the old and the sick" and "perhaps even the middle class."[25] In the face of sustained public opposition, Reagan backed away. What stands out about Reagan, however, is that he persisted in many cases with policies that were unpopular with the general public but that he and his core supporters backed.

Archival records and empirical research reveal how Reagan pursued a strategy that was persistently conservative unless he wished to prevent a damaging backlash by swing voters; Nixon adopted an approach that was more sensitive to the median voter but alert for tactical opportunities to quell potential conservative revolts. As Nixon relied on his private polling to carefully track mainstream America, Reagan used his polling to cater to the diverse set of social, economic, and military conservative forces that formed his electoral coalition, pulling back (as in the case of Social Security reform) on the occasions where White House data detected significant defections among swing voters.

## The Politics of Information Collection and Use

Previous research claimed that imperfect information instills uncertainty among politicians who tip-toe around voters to avoid alienating them and refrain from risking policy goals that vividly diverge from their opponent's (Shepsle 1972; Page 1978). Neglected is the extensive information about the type of public opinion that presidents have assembled to fit their political needs and used to minimize the risk of pursuing the policy goals that they and their loyalists favor.

Where past research on imperfect information concluded that politicians quell their policy goals to minimize risk, our original analysis finds that presidents scientifically map risk in order to narrow their responsiveness to the broad public to a few salient issues that voters scrutinize and to widen their discretion to pursue their policy goals. Reagan relied on his sophisticated polling to cater to conservatives until it flagged (as in the case of his far-reaching proposal to privatize Social Security) a substantial risk of alienating swing voters. Nixon took a more opportunistic approach of using his polling to pinpoint openings of voter disinterest to stake out conservative positions that quieted his restless base.

Leveraging their extensive polling information, presidents add a second precaution for pursuing policy goals—they attempt to shift the focus of voters to nonpolicy considerations related to personality. As we show in a later chapter, the White House seeks to prime the president's image and to distract voters from scrutinizing his policy agenda.

The overarching theme of the White House's collection and use of private polls is its attentiveness not to the broad public (as research on political representation has long assumed) but to particular segments of the electorate—a theme the next chapter examines in greater depth.

### CHAPTER FOUR

# Segmented Representation

Who is represented? Presidents have long portrayed themselves as "stewards of the people" who serve the entire country and its greater good (Gerring 1998; Bimes and Mulroy 2004). Modern presidents (with the assent of political science) regularly present themselves and their policies as reflecting the national interest, in contrast to recalcitrant members of Congress, who act on behalf of narrow, well-organized factions (Tulis 1987; Kernell 1986/2006; Moe 1993).

Presidential promotion of the greater good channels a deep yearning first crystalized by the framers of the US Constitution in the Federalist Papers. They argued that "the People *commonly intend* the public good"[1] but their passions and myopia make them unreliable and susceptible to the whims and interests of "factions" who threaten the "permanent and aggregate interests of the community." The antidote was to rely on the wisdom of government officials who "may best discern the true interest of their country and [are] . . . least likely to sacrifice it to temporary or partial considerations."[2] The president's position as the nation's ceremonial head, commander in chief, and sole occupant of the executive branch selected by an independent electoral college was expected to give him the resources and incentives to serve the country's overall well-being. Where legislators were motivated to protect the narrow interests of constituents in their districts or states, presidents were expected to secure the interests of the nation as a whole.[3]

Following the Constitution's ratification, presidents promoted themselves to tap into Americans' deep cultural yearning for common purpose (Mansbridge 1990). They presented their policies as expressing the country's "civic republican" virtue and enduring commitment to the collective possibilities of politics (Wood 1969; Sandel 1996). In contemporary

America, they often call on voters to look beyond their own pocketbooks by casting electoral votes based on the state of the national economy, which empirical research confirms as a common pattern in voting behavior (Kinder and Kiewiet 1981; Mutz and Mondak 1997).

The self-promotional efforts of presidents to equate themselves with the best interests of the nation are evident in the scholarly study of political representation, which focuses on the government's relationship with largely undifferentiated populations: the attitudes of the mass public in a congressional district, state, or nation (Miller and Stokes 1963; Page and Shapiro 1983; Erikson, MacKuen, and Stimson 2002). Systematic differences in how officeholders might treat distinct policy domains (economic, social, and foreign) are also neglected even though pressures from constituents and lobbyists might vary (but see Wlezien 2004).

The portrayal of presidents as the embodiment of the nation by the White House and accommodating scholars neglects, however, a central feature of this branch of American politics—their selective attention to special interests and political loyalists and their strategies to mobilize them as supporters. Much of the study of political representation has become oddly apolitical and disinterested in inequalities in influence even though ample evidence shows that distinct subgroups of citizens, particularly the wealthy and certain engaged groups, participate in elections and a range of other political activities at far higher rates than do others (Verba, Schlozman, and Brady 1995). A comprehensive political analysis of representation needs to connect the disparities in influence to elite strategies that aim to cultivate segments of the electorate through poll-crafted communications and mobilize and recruit new constituents, as Lisa Disch (2011) cogently explains (see also Manin 1997).

Presidents' strategy of recasting political representation to widen their policy discretion is geared to selectively responding to two segments of American society. The first aspect of segmented representation is aimed at tailoring policy to affluent individuals, organizations, and businesses (Bartels 2008; Gilens 2005; Jacobs and Page 2005; Gilens and Page, in press; Enns and Wlezien 2011). The second aspect has received less attention: the disproportionate influence on government officials of social and political subgroups *not* directly defined by economic advantage, such as religious groups or ideological issue publics (Wood 2009).

This chapter capitalizes on private archival records from the Reagan White House to examine its distinctive strategies to mobilize segments of the electorate through differentiated appeals within particular policy domains. As we will explain, Reagan entered office during a critical political period highlighted by the demise of the Democrats' New Deal coalition. This led the White House to construct a strategy aimed at building a new conservative Republican coalition that included high-income earners and groups organized to promote particular issue agendas. On the one hand, the administration worked to lock in its base of support among Republicans, military and fiscal conservatives, and the affluent. On the other hand, it sought to extend the Party's traditional base to political independents and to social conservatives who had often been disconnected from American politics as a coherent force. Our analyses demonstrate that presidents publicly claim to serve the nation but that their administrations work diligently to cater to segments of the country—the clusters of voters who are most prone to deliver reliable support.

## Going Narrow

The early 1970s was a period of significant change in the electorate and the organization of political parties and their process for selecting candidates. One result was the substantially greater influence of single-issue and ideologically extreme party activists. Within the Republican Party, social conservatives (especially born-again Protestants and Baptist fundamentalists), economic conservatives (especially supply-side advocates favoring sharp reductions in government taxation), and philosophical conservatives all gained new prominence in candidate selection and in government circles (Aldrich 1995; Edsall and Edsall 1991). Even as ideologically oriented party activists gained more sway, both political parties competed to appeal to the growing ranks of independent voters, who often swung election outcomes. As the Democratic Party's New Deal coalition unraveled and stalwart supporters such as Catholics drifted from the party, the proportion of voters who described themselves as independent in surveys conducted by American National Election Studies rose from 23 percent in 1952 to 34 percent by 1980.[4]

These significant changes in the electorate and in party organization generated incentives for national political leaders to win over politically critical segments of the electorate. With leaders in both parties maneuvering for advantage, Republican politicians were motivated to construct a new conservative coalition—one that would expand Barry Goldwater's economic libertarianism to include social conservatives, supply-siders who favored sharply lower taxes (even at the risk of higher budget deficits), and philosophical conservatives. They also were motivated to draw in independents fleeing the collapsing New Deal coalition, which had long been a foundation of domestic policy. Reagan White House officials described their project of connecting with distinct but often estranged groups of conservatives and disaffected parts of the old Democratic coalition as "the keys to any permanent realignment."[5]

Put simply, Republicans and the Reagan team embraced an ambitious political project of stitching together distinct economic and political segments of the electorate. In particular, they aimed to unite (*a*) political independents, (*b*) high-income groups, (*c*) social conservatives (namely, fundamentalist Baptists and Catholics as they defected from the Democratic Party), and (*d*) philosophical conservatives who constituted the Republican Party base.[6]

## Practicing Segmented Representation

Archival records provide a clear portrait of how the incentive to construct a new coalition of subgroups shaped the Reagan White House's polling efforts. As explained in chapter 2, the Reagan administration focused intently on the "characteristics of voters" in order to monitor the voters that formed Reagan's base of support.[7] It was attuned to the electoral segments that favored the president, improving its capacity to focus its resources and strategies on specific election contests and legislative battles.[8]

In its polling the White House targeted those segments of the electorate that formed the "core Reagan support group[s]." For instance, the Reagan team assembled little data on middle- and lower-income groups as it focused intently on gathering information about the affluent. It also gave particular attention to the segments of the electorate that "took Reagan over the top in 1980"—especially, political independents and individuals who leaned independent, including weak Democrats and moderates.[9]

The Republican Party loyalists who formed Reagan's base of support were another target of White House polling. However, the president's advisers (including the pollster Richard Wirthlin) recognized that political conservatives "alone do not constitute an electoral majority."[10] The search for allies led to the concerted tracking of social conservatives—especially Baptists and Catholics.

The White House's use of these segmented data was reflected in Wirthlin's parsing of what he presented as "aggregate" polling results. He disaggregated results to spotlight Reagan's area of "strength" ("base Republicans") and "swing" voters—independents and leaners as well as Baptists and Catholics.[11] As part of this focus on discrete segments of the electorate, Reagan tracked their policy preferences across a range of issues—supplying a steady supply of Policy Opinion data on the percentage of individuals who took a position on a given issue.

Archival evidence suggests that Reagan's skepticism about aggregate results in favor of subgroup breakdowns manifested itself in his political strategy. For instance, when White House polling showed that majorities had shifted toward favoring cuts in defense spending to reduce the federal government budget deficit, Reagan's team discounted the findings because "those who are most in favor of [it] . . . (postgraduates, liberals, blacks, Deep South residents, college graduates, and non-married women) are not our strength constituency." Instead, staff focused on "swing and strength constituencies . . . [and especially] swing groups—White Baptists, blue-collar workers, Catholics."[12] Similarly, Gary Bauer (who later became a Republican Party presidential candidate and prominent social conservative advocate) forcefully argued: "When we are on the 'wrong' side of . . . issues from a [general] public opinion standpoint . . . [Reagan's position] still may be politically positive." In particular, he pointed to Reagan's opposition to abortion as a critical draw for urban Catholics who had spurned Democrats because they were "associated with abortion on demand."[13] Staff debates over how—and whether—to attend to subgroup opinion were wired into the White House organization, which assigned particular staff and offices to tracking the attitudes of these clusters of voters and to actively maintaining ties to their leaders.

Polling of subgroups prompted not only policy initiatives but also nonaction. For instance, Wirthlin reported that legislation granting amnesty to illegal immigrants "carrie[d] liabilities for the President" because "elements of our key constituents are on both sides of the issue." "The best political solution," he counseled, "is deadlocking the bill in [the] conference committee."[14]

## White House Polling of Subgroups

Reagan's segmented strategy focused the White House on both politically significant subgroups and the particular issues and policy domains they most valued. Archival records point to four possible tactics, which we will test shortly—focusing on the degree to which its strategic intentions influenced the use by the White House of polling to fashion Reagan's policy statements and position taking. First, the White House's internal discussions indicate that its courting of affluent Americans will focus Reagan's position taking on their intense concern with specific economic issues. In terms of how the White House's polling is used, Reagan's team is expected to be acutely responsive to higher-income groups when fashioning his public position on taxes, government spending, and Social Security (e.g., opposition to expanding or even maintaining Social Security).

Second, the White House's efforts to draw new swing groups—mainly Baptists and Catholics—into an expanded conservative coalition are expected to exert a disproportionately strong influence on Reagan's specific positions on conservative social policies relating to family values and crime. Third, the administration's attention to the Republican base is expected to influence Reagan's public positions on defense spending—an issue long seen as one that the Republicans "own" (e.g., Petrocik 1996). Fourth, the White House's courting of the political independents who were falling away from the New Deal coalition is expected to create strong incentives for it to concentrate on their preferences for specific domestic policies. Focusing on domestic issues close to daily life (as opposed to distant matters abroad) is likely to connect with independent voters, who tend to be less informed and interested in politics than are partisans and other identifiable political groups (Delli Carpini and Keeter 1996).

The White House consistently decided to collect Policy Opinion data on these four areas of intense subgroup interest.[15] Overall, 71 percent of the White House's domestic issue polling broke out the finding into one or more subgroups. Results for different income groups were reported 46 percent of the time, with 34 percent of these instances devoted to the core economic issues related to taxes, government spending, and Social Security. As suggested by the White House's discussion of strategy, its polling was targeted on detecting the views of the highest-income earners on these issues; 84 percent of polling on core economic issues that provided results by income groups also included specific data regarding the affluent.[16] Additionally, on domestic issues, the White House broke out results for Baptists or Catholics 53 percent of the time. Fifteen percent of these data were on the social conservative issues of family values and crime that were potentially of particular interest to these subgroups. Finally, across both domestic and foreign policy domains, the White House collected data on the specific views of its political base—Republicans—65 percent of the time; its polling on defense spending broke down the data on Republican attitudes 99 percent of the time.

## Reagan Caters to Factions

How did Reagan's polling on politically significant subgroups and their issue agendas affect the White House's political strategy in practice? As in the previous chapter, in this one we explore this question by examining the relationship between the White House's polling and the president's policy positions, which are coded on a five-point scale with higher scores indicating an increasingly conservative position (standardized to a 0–1 scale). The White House polling data measure the percentage of respondents taking a conservative position on an issue at least one month prior to a statement; we standardize these data to 0–1 scales (for the regression analyses, 0 = 0 percent, and 1 = 100 percent and the most conservative position). As in chapter 3, our data here span ninety-eight issues over ninety-seven months; there is a drop-off in the number of cases owing to missing data.

In table 4.1, we describe Reagan's positions and the White House's Policy Opinion by issue areas in terms of average scores and subgroup attitudes.[17] The most consistent pattern is that Reagan generally took conservative positions. What stands out, however, is that he was near the extreme point of the scale on social conservative policies and defense spending. Merely eyeballing the White House's polling data on politically targeted subgroups shows a similar conservative tilt: most notably, virtually all Baptists polled endorsed conservative social policies. Conversely, the attitudes of independents on domestic issues were less conservative. (Recall that these public opinion data reflect the choices of the Reagan White House with regard to specific issues and should not be read as general public sentiment during Reagan's tenure.)

Did the distinctive attitudes of politically significant subgroups affect Reagan's behavior? To investigate this question, we follow the general approach used in chapter 3 of regressing the president's Policy Positions on lagged values of key control variables[18] with an important addition—we include variables for the lagged Policy Opinions of the key subgroups presented in table 4.1. For example, when exploring Reagan's tax positions, we include the lagged Policy Opinion variable reflecting the percentage of all respondents who favor cutting taxes as well as a variable to capture

TABLE 4.1  **Descriptive Data by Issue Area**

| Issue Area | Reagan's Average Position[a] | Overall Average Policy Opinion[b] | Subgroup Average Policy Opinion[b] | |
|---|---|---|---|---|
| Domestic policy (*N* = 847) | 3.37 (1.83) | .49 (.26) | Independents .47 (.30) | |
| Economic policy (Social Security, taxes, spending) (*N* = 173) | 4.21 (1.40) | .55 (.21) | High Income .68 (.12) | |
| | | | Catholics | Baptists |
| Social conservative policy (family values, crime) (*N* = 104) | 4.97 (.14) | .78 (.13) | .87 (.06) | .90 (.05) |
| Defense spending (*N* = 90) | 4.84 (.50) | .53 (.12) | Republicans .70 (.11) | |

*Note*: Standard deviations are given in parentheses.

[a] Measured on a scale of 1–5 with higher scores indicating increased conservativeness.

[b] Percentage supporting a conservative position.

the specific percentage of high-income earners who favor cutting taxes.[19] Because our opinion data are coded in a congruent direction with Reagan's positions, a significant positive coefficient suggests that the president adjusts his positions to trends in opinions. We studied this relationship for the policy areas of greatest concern to the four subgroups targeted by the White House (high-income earners, independents, fundamental Baptists and Catholics, and Republicans). We were generally unable to conduct this analysis more comprehensively: the administration concentrated both on key subgroups (rarely providing data on other segments such as middle- or low-income earners) and on the issues of greatest interest to these subgroups (often neglecting their wider set of attitudes, such as the economic attitudes of social conservative voters).

Our analysis begins with independents, which White House strategists identified as potentially receptive to the president's discussion of domestic issues if he was sensitive to their views. Table 4.2 reveals notable effects of political independents on Reagan's domestic positions. The results show that general Policy Opinions are statistically significant but that the public's Ideological Identification is not. Importantly, the policy preferences of independents were substantially stronger than the policy preferences of the general public (.40 versus .17; statistically significant). Here is a more direct gauge of the greater effect of independents. When the *general*

TABLE 4.2  **Impact of the Policy Preferences of Independents on Domestic Policy
Positions (Dependent Variable: Presidential Policy Positions on Domestic Policy)**

| Independent Variables | OLS Coefficients | Standard Errors |
| --- | --- | --- |
| Public's ideological identification | −.04 | .30 |
| Public's policy opinions | .17** | .06 |
| Policy opinions of independents | .40** | .06 |
| Presidential policy positions, $t-1$ | .56** | .03 |
| Constant | .01 | .18 |
| $R^2$ | .74 | ... |
| $N$ | 847 | ... |

** $p \leq .05$, * $p \leq .10$, one-tailed test.

*public* moved its opinions from 10 percent below its mean to 10 percent
over its mean (in a conservative direction), Reagan moved his position,
on average, in a conservative direction by 3.5 percent.[20] While this is not
trivial, it is even more impressive that, when the opinions of *independents*
moved from 10 percent below to 10 percent above the mean, Reagan's
positions became 8 percent more conservative on average.

The magnitude of Reagan's adjustment of his position in response to
independent voters is impressive given the potent controls that we included[21] and the well-documented inertia in policy positions (e.g., Erikson, MacKuen, and Stimson 2002, 285). His greater attention to independent voters, relative to voters in general, accentuates the privileged status
of independents where domestic issues were concerned, as spelled out by
administration strategists.[22]

White House strategists also targeted high-income earners as a core
constituency to please on the economic issues of concern to them—taxes,
spending, and Social Security. Our analyses investigated the impact on
Reagan of the affluent on these core economic issues.

Table 4.3 confirms the striking impact of high-income earners on
Reagan's economic policies. The public's Ideological Identification is not
statistically significant; the White House did not tailor Reagan's public
statements on core economic issues to an overriding conservatism among
Americans. Instead, those statements were driven by the public's Policy
Opinions on these issues, but much more strongly by the views of the
most affluent. When the general public's opinions shift from 10 percent
below to 10 percent above the average, Reagan became 3.5 percent more
conservative, compared to a whopping 20 percent more conservative for
an analogous move among the affluent (controlling for Ideological Identification and the president's prior opinion). Put simply, these results dem-

onstrate that Reagan clearly paid dramatic attention to the views of the wealthy on economic issues.

The third politically significant subgroup pursued by the White House was socially conservative Baptists and Catholics who harbored strong views about family values and a law-and-order approach to crime. Table 4.4, which presents regressions on these issues and includes the Policy Opinions of Baptists and Catholics, indicates that Reagan did not systematically tailor his comments on social conservative policies to Policy Opinions in general or specifically to Catholics. However, the social conservative policy preferences of Baptists notably registered as a statistically significant influence on Reagan's statements. Substantively, when Baptists shift from 10 percent below to 10 percent above the average opinion, Reagan's positions become 7 percent more conservative.

What stands out about social conservative policies is that Reagan appeared to be adopting entirely new positions in reaction to the preferences of Baptists. In particular, the statistical insignificance of the lagged

TABLE 4.3 **Impact of the Policy Preferences of High-Income Americans on Economic Policy Positions (Dependent Variable: Reagan's Policy Positions on Social Security Reform, Lower Taxes, Government Spending)**

| Independent Variables | OLS Coefficients | Standard Errors |
|---|---|---|
| Public's ideological identification | −.11 | .40 |
| Public's policy opinions | .18** | .09 |
| Policy opinions of higher-income Americans | 1.01** | .21 |
| Presidential policy positions, $t-1$ | .50** | .07 |
| Constant | −.32 | .27 |
| $R^2$ | .84 | ... |
| $N$ | 173 | ... |

** $p \leq .05$, * $p \leq .10$, one-tailed test.

TABLE 4.4 **Impact of the Policy Preferences of Baptists and Catholics on Social Conservative Policy Positions (Dependent Variable: Reagan's Policy Positions on Family Values and Crime)**

| Independent Variables | OLS Coefficients | Standard Errors |
|---|---|---|
| Public's ideological identification | −.03 | .13 |
| Public's policy opinions | −.06 | .05 |
| Policy opinions of Baptists | .35** | .21 |
| Policy opinions of Catholics | −.07 | .17 |
| Presidential policy positions, $t-1$ | −.11 | .10 |
| Constant | .92** | .15 |
| $R^2$ | .07 | ... |
| $N$ | 104 | ... |

** $p \leq .05$, * $p \leq .10$, one-tailed test.

TABLE 4.5  **Impact of the Policy Preferences of Republicans on Defense Spending Policy Positions (Dependent Variable: Reagan's Policy Positions on Increased Defense Spending)**

| Independent Variables | OLS Coefficients | Standard Errors |
|---|---|---|
| Public's ideological identification | .83* | .53 |
| Public's policy opinions | −.08 | .11 |
| Policy opinions of Republicans | 1.25** | .43 |
| Policy opinions of independents | −.97** | .38 |
| Policy opinions of Democrats | −.52* | .32 |
| Presidential policy positions, $t-1$ | −.03 | .10 |
| Constant | .53* | .39 |
| $R^2$ | .15 | . . . |
| $N$ | 90 | . . . |

** $p \leq .05$, * $p \leq .10$, one-tailed test.

dependent variable suggests that his previous positions did not lock in his comments. These statistical results, along with archival records, confirm that Reagan viewed Baptists as an especially important group for expanding the party's conservative base.

As the Reagan team worked to expand its coalition, it remained focused on maintaining the support of philosophically conservative Republicans. In line with Reagan's own predilections, these voters were intent on strengthening national security and increasing defense spending. Table 4.5 expands on our analysis in chapter 3 demonstrating that the White House relied on ideological data on foreign and defense policy to cater to the concerns of conservatives. It reconfirms our earlier findings: the ideological mood of the electorate influenced defense spending positions. More importantly, the results reveal that Reagan closely tailored his public comments on defense spending to the views of Republicans; the size of this impact exceeded that of general conservative ideology. When Republican opinion shifted from 10 percent below to 10 percent above the average, Reagan moved by 25 percent.

Unlike what we have seen in our prior subgroup analyses, on defense spending Reagan did collect sufficient other subgroup data to make it possible to include the Policy Opinions of independents and Democrats. Underscoring his ideological orientation, the opinions of independents and Democrats are significant but negative: he moved substantially away from them.[23] In short, Reagan honed his public statements on defense spending to signal his attentiveness to partisans and conservatives and his determination to mobilize them while turning against other segments of the electorate.

## Reagan's Conservative Coalition

Much of the empirical study of political representation has focused on whether government responds to general public opinion and concluded that politicians generally follow the median voter (Downs 1957). This democratic responsiveness account rests on the expectation that government officials—and presidents in particular—represent the nation as a whole against special interests (Moe 1993). Reagan captured this alluring portrayal of national responsiveness in his first swearing-in ceremony in 1981: "Our loyalty must be only to this Nation and to the people that we represent. I've often said the only people in Washington who represent *all the people* are those, basically, that are found here, because we're beholden to no district, beholden to no particular section of State" (quoted in Wood 2009, 14).

In practice, however, the commitment of presidents to the policies backed by core political and economic interests produces two departures from the expectation of democratic responsiveness. First, as we will demonstrate in the next chapter, they seek to move public opinion to support the policies that they and their supporters favor rather than passively following what the median voter prefers. Treating public opinion as an autonomous driver of policy neglects the substantial efforts that political elites make to shape it.

Second, this chapter's evidence of the impacts of special interests contradicts Reagan's soaring inaugural promise to "represent *all the people*" and the optimism of pluralists that "any active and legitimate group will make itself heard effectively at some stage in the process of decision" (Dahl 1956, 149–51). An innovative combination of archival evidence and quantitative analysis demonstrates that the Reagan administration routinely tracked segments of the country that it deemed politically important and fashioned its positions to appeal to their most intense policy preferences.

Reagan's two-track strategy is geared to mobilizing and recruiting new constituencies and reenergizing old ones. One component of his segmentation was his disproportionate attention to the preferences of the highest-income earners. This pattern is compatible with extensive and long-standing research about the asymmetrical distribution of resources among citizens, organizations, and groups and the biasing effects it has on government policy (Beard 1913; McConnell 1966; Mills 1956; Schattschneider 1960). Evidence of the particular sway of the wealthy over the

Reagan administration is also consistent with a new generation of research that links rising economic inequality with political disparities (American Political Science Association Task Force 2004; Bartels 2008; Gilens 2012; Jacobs and Page 2005; Jacobs and Skocpol 2005b). Reagan's plan to rely on segmentation was attentive not only to the affluent but also to religious conservatives as well as to the Republican Party's base.

The second component of the Reagan White House's strategic use of private polling to track electorally significant subgroups was geared to a reshaping of contemporary American politics. Its careful calibration of the president's public positions to reflect the White House's subgroup polling contributed to the formation of a new and broader conservative coalition—one that strengthened its appeal among the affluent, philosophical conservatives and Goldwater-type economic libertarians while also widening it to political independents and religious conservatives. Social conservatives (especially born-again Protestants and Baptist fundamentalists), economic conservatives (especially supply-side advocates favoring sharp reductions in government taxation), and philosophical conservatives all gained new prominence in the coalition that Reagan constructed. His cultivation of a diverse conservative coalition created sustained pathways to government policy for the most advantaged economic interests in a period of rising economic inequality (Hacker and Pierson 2010).

### CHAPTER FIVE

# Elite Strategies to Prime Issues and Image

D o government officials treat citizens as the masters to serve? According to agency theory, voters are expected to serve as "principals" who control their "agents" in government (Fearon 1999; Miller 2005). The responsiveness account adopts the primary expectation of principal-agent models: officeholders are expected to be "scared" by the prospect of electoral defeat into studiously following the preferences of citizens (Erikson, MacKuen, and Stimson 2002; Downs 1957; Mayhew 1974).

Rather than accepting public attitudes as a restriction on their decisions, the president and his senior aides attempt to change the electorate's views in order to create leeway to pursue the policy goals that they and their loyal supporters favor. Presidents have fused their unrivaled capacities for communications and private polling to develop potent, but realistic, strategies for shaping public opinion (Jacobs and Shapiro 1994). This process began with the administration of Lyndon Johnson and took on greater sophistication during the presidencies of Richard Nixon and Ronald Reagan.

Presidents and their political advisers learned a key lesson from their predecessors: even the White House's new capacities for honed communications could not routinely mold public opinion like clay (as demonstrated by the struggles of Lyndon Johnson and, later, Richard Nixon to stem the rising tide of public opposition to them). White House aides did discover, however, a more limited but realistic strategy: they used their capacities to prime Americans to pay particular attention to selected issues for two purposes—to prod them to focus attention on issues that they already supported and to promote particularly compelling images of the president (such as strength or competence) in order to influence evaluations of him. This approach accepts that presidents are often unable to dominate public debate (as naive political observers continue to expect [e.g., Westen 2011]). Instead, strategic presidents attempt to leverage their influence over the public's agenda of issues to create a potentially potent tool both for blame avoidance by highlighting certain issues to distract attention from unpopular policies and for credit claiming by driving attention to advantageous issues and personality traits.

As presidents were developing their communications strategies, a body of research independently formed that investigated similar dynamics—namely, the political effects of "priming" to achieve finely targeted agenda setting (Miller and Krosnick 2000). Priming research offers an analytic framework for explaining how presidents exert substantial—if targeted—influence on the public by strategically crafting their statements to raise the salience of selected policy issues and to affect the public's personal image of them—what we refer to as *issue priming* and *image priming*, respectively.

We explore the presidential strategy of priming to engage in credit claiming and blame avoidance by investigating Nixon and Reagan. White House polling reports of strong public support for particular domestic policy positions prompted both presidents to subsequently increase their statements on that issue, thereby drawing more attention to areas of strength. Conversely, they sought to avoid attracting blame by highlighting more advantageous issues to distract public scrutiny and by minimizing discussion of vexing issues and unpopular positions—such as the unavoidably salient Vietnam War. In addition, poll reports of negative evaluations of the president's personality traits led the White House to select issues, such as foreign policy or the economy, in order to bolster positive impressions of his personality. These general patterns, moreover, are conditioned by the parameters of public opinion and by prevailing circumstances confronting presidents.

## Explaining Presidential Priming

We generate a framework for studying elite issue and image priming by synthesizing three themes in existing research on political psychology, election campaigns, and elite mobilization. First, we directly link political communications and private polling to pinpoint how political actors and, specifically, presidents tailor their statements to prime Americans.

This breaks into the black box of presumed strategizing that characterizes much previous research (e.g., Riker 1996; Sellers 1998). Second, we add a new dimension to elite priming strategy—namely, the effort to elevate the salience of certain *image* perceptions or personality traits (see also Druckman and Holmes 2004). This corrects for the tendency in prior research to focus almost exclusively on the attempts of political elites to activate policy issues and ignore efforts to strategically use priming to influence image perception, which holds the potential to shift political representation away from substantive policy. Third, we treat priming as a thoroughly political strategy. We link how political elites design and implement their priming strategies to the incentive structures of elections and the struggle for influence over policy in three respects—existing public evaluations of policy issues, the perceived personality of political elites, and independent or exogenous real-world events that can shape the public agenda.

## Issue Priming

Analysts have paid a great deal of attention to election campaigns and the impact of political strategies on voting and public opinion over the past two decades. They have converged on priming as a process for exerting influence that is substantial in impact, even if more limited than persuading, or potentially manipulating, individuals to drop one set of core policy preferences for another. Priming is a process whereby individuals come to place more emphasis, or weight, on a set of issues as they evaluate candidates (Johnston, Blais, Brady, and Crete 1992) or presidents (Jacobs and Shapiro 1994; Iyengar and Kinder 1987). Priming effects can be triggered by the media or political elites.

Priming research has broadened from examining its influence on voters to investigating how campaigns use it as a strategy (e.g., Riker 1996; Jacobs and Shapiro 1994). The strategic goal is not to change basic policy preferences per se but to alter how voters evaluate a particular policy or politician by emphasizing selected issues in order to induce individuals to increase their attention to those issues and the stored set of attitudes associated with them (Berelson, Lazarsfeld, and McPhee 1954, 253–73; Jacobs and Shapiro 1994; Jacoby 1998; Johnston, Blais, Brady, and Crete 1992; Page 1978; Petrocik 1996; Riker 1996; Sellers 1998). For example, an incumbent president with a booming jobs market may emphasize the economy in his public comments to prime voters to base their evaluations of him on this issue rather than some other (Druckman 2004).

that asked respondents to identify their general feelings toward Reagan; the administration treated this as an additional way to gauge warmth. The Nixon administration rarely tracked thermometer ratings, and, thus, we do not include it in those analyses; they do not appear to have received much routine attention. Higher scores on each scale meant an increase in the given trait. White House polls also tracked a general measure of *conservatism* as another important aspect of the president's image. Our analysis is restricted to Reagan's first term as his administration virtually stopped image polling after the 1984 election.

To analyze these data, we created monthly aggregated measures of each of the three sets of variables. For each month for which data were available, we created measures of the public's policy attitudes on each of forty-nine issues for Nixon and ninety-eight for Reagan (as measured by approval of the president's policy performance, support for his policy position on each issue, and importance ranking) as well as of the public's evaluations of the image variables—competence, strength, warmth, trust, and conservatism. As we discussed in chapter 2, this creates 2,303 possible observations for Nixon (forty-nine issues over twenty-seven months) and 9,506 potential observations for Reagan (ninety-eight issues over ninety-seven months), though the actual number of observations is consistently smaller owing to missing data. The administration did not collect data for each type of survey question for the full set of policy issues over the entire time period. The sample sizes for the image analyses are always significantly larger than for our issue analyses because they are general and apply across any type of presidential statement; by contrast, the pool of issue questions is smaller because they are specifically compared to statements in those specific domains.

In our analyses, we used time lags for the polling data to capture the time required for the survey organizations to enter and analyze their results, for the White House to consider the results and incorporate them into its strategy, and for the lingering effect of polling results before the next batch of survey findings arrived. Records suggest that the White House used the previous set of results, even if this meant going back in time.

Our quantitative analyses regress the amount of space that the presidents devote to core policy issues on the White House's polling data regarding issues and then image. This allows us to evaluate whether Nixon and Reagan engaged in priming by emphasizing issues or personality traits (or in some cases both).[14] We use negative binomial regression because our dependent variable—the space presidents devote to discussing issues in their public statements—is an event count.[15] Interpreting coefficients in the case of a negative binomial is never straightforward—and even more so in our case given that we scale our independent variables from 0 to 1 but leave space limitless because it is theoretically not finite. In some cases, as will be clear, this leads to what appear to be extraordinarily large coefficients because of large variance on the space-dependent variable and much less on the independent variables; in these cases, we will aim to clarify the results to show the actual—more realistic—effects.

In order to pinpoint the White House's motivation and strategy, we supplement quantitative research, which identifies central tendencies, with archival records and other historical evidence. Internal debates within the Nixon and Reagan administrations often differentiated domestic and foreign affairs as well as more fine-tuned distinctions in the White House's communications. In the Reagan White House, for instance, polling data were distributed on the basis of policy responsibilities; National Security Adviser John Poindexter received the latest data on foreign policy, while aides specializing in domestic policies received data relevant to their domains (Eisinger 2003, 163–64). The White House's incorporation of polling in its decision-making process guided our quantitative research decision to examine the full range of policies together as well as to separate out domestic and foreign policy. This multimethod approach steered us, for instance, toward exploring Nixon's possible inclination to calibrate his issue priming on the basis of policy domain, focusing on domestic affairs while steering clear of Vietnam and foreign affairs.

*Priming in Practice*

Archival research and statistical analysis document that Nixon and Reagan pursued issue and image priming in ways that were attuned to existing public attitudes and real-world circumstances. We now explore the four expectations that we identified earlier.

EVIDENCE FOR ISSUE PRIMING.    We begin by examining issue priming. Internal White House strategizing and past research suggests, as discussed above, that Nixon and Reagan engaged in issue priming only for domestic issues. There was little sense to investing scarce time priming foreign affairs when White House polls showed Vietnam and the Cold War were already consistently at the top of voters' minds.

These expectations are strongly supported in table 5.1, which reports the regression results for Nixon and Reagan (for each issue variable) in

TABLE 5.1  **Effects of White House Issue Polling on the Space of Nixon and Reagan's Statements**

|  | All Issues | Domestic | Foreign |
|---|---|---|---|
| Approval of president's policy performance: | | | |
| Nixon | −.89 | −1.72 | 4.38** |
|  | (1.24) | (1.43) | (2.50) |
| Reagan | 1.42 | −1.12 | −3.27 |
|  | (1.76) | (3.06) | (2.66) |
| Support for president's policy positions: | | | |
| Nixon | 3.11** | 4.28** | −5.63 |
|  | (1.57) | (1.79) | (8.07) |
| Reagan | 1.27** | 2.31** | −.377 |
|  | (.47) | (.69) | (.68) |
| Issue importance: | | | |
| Nixon | .55 | .95 | 4.83 |
|  | (2.20) | (4.17) | (3.92) |
| Reagan | −4.42** | .74 | −13.47** |
|  | (1.9) | (2.65) | (2.97) |
| Constant: | | | |
| Nixon | 3.22* | 3.09** | 5.28** |
|  | (.59) | (.82) | (5.25) |
| Reagan | 3.56** | 2.83** | 6.08** |
|  | (.45) | (.61) | (.75) |
| α (alpha): | | | |
| Nixon | 2.44** | 2.66** | 1.26** |
|  | (.27) | (.34) | (.31) |
| Reagan | 3.28** | 3.44** | 2.55** |
|  | (.19) | (.24) | (.24) |
| N: | | | |
| Nixon | 182 | 153 | 29 |
| Reagan | 608 | 403 | 205 |
| Log likelihood: | | | |
| Nixon | −921.26 | −747.90 | −167.69 |
| Reagan | −2,908.76 | −1,805.64 | −1,083.00 |

*Note:* Entries are negative binomial regression coefficients with standard errors in parentheses. ** $p \leq .01$, * $p \leq .05$, one-tailed test. Dependent variable is the space that each president devoted to publicly speaking on selected issues.

the rows across all issues, then just domestic issues, and then just foreign affairs. Both engaged in issue priming across all issues: the significant coefficients for priming of all issues are 3.11 for Nixon and 1.27 for Reagan. Their priming of issues is consistent with Riker's (1986) claim that it is position taking that matters and not approval per se or issue. The two Republican presidents apparently anticipated voters casting their ballots for the candidate who agrees with them on positions rather than looking toward importance or general approval.[16] In fact, Reagan appeared to prime/emphasize issues (such as his aggressive interventions in Central America) even if the public failed to rank them as important (a significant −4.42 on all issues).

The results also strongly support our hypothesis that issue priming was focused on the domain of domestic affairs. Nixon and Reagan attempted to prime domestic issues on which the public supported their positions with the hope of inducing voters to focus on these issues (significant coefficients of 4.28 and 2.31, respectively). There is only scant evidence that either president invested in priming foreign policy. Nixon devoted more space to foreign policy based not on issue approval but on general approval; he may have been attempting to broaden the discussion of foreign affairs to dissipate the attention on Vietnam when he was popular (we did not anticipate this, but it is not a surprising finding per se). Reagan apparently did not feel the need to do so with regard to the Cold War given its general popularity. In short, the major result of priming of popular domestic issues confirms each president's efforts to credit claim.

Our analysis also confirms that Reagan singled out relatively nonsalient foreign policies (significant coefficient of −13.47). This reflects his ideological commitment to the administration's unpopular agenda in Nicaragua.[17]

Memoranda and other material from the Nixon White House reinforce the findings of our quantitative analysis. Haldeman's diary pointed to polling as determining "whether *our position* [on specific issues] has gone up or down in the eyes of the public."[18] Nixon and his aides calculated that highlighting "issues where the President is favorably received" would make "Americans realize that the President is with them on these issues" and counteract the opposition's "attempt to capitalize on the mood of a substantial portion of the electorate . . . [that] the government isn't concerned or responsive."[19] Reagan's memoranda provide a similar portrait—his main pollster, Wirthlin, recommended priming the economy and the administration's program for revitalizing it: "An aggressive program of presidential events, statements and surrogate support for a balanced budget amendment would improve the approval ratings." Wirthlin also warned the president when not to prime an issue on which the public did not support his position: "By raising the political stakes and public salience of [aiding Nicaragua], you would . . . put into jeopardy the favorable job approval you now enjoy" (quoted in Eisinger 2003, 166). In this case, Reagan's ideological compulsions overrode this practical advice—a puzzle we explore further below.

Our statistical research and qualitative research present the first rigorous evidence of how presidents use their private polls to prime issues to their advantage. In particular, Nixon's and Reagan's careful tracking of their minds, as supporters commonly urge presidents, was a naive tactic for exercising predictable influence. Instead, Nixon and Reagan turned to tracking public opinion to improve their potential to exert influence.

Nixon and Reagan advanced a particular strategy for guiding public opinion, what we call *issue priming* and *image priming*, one that targeted topics at the forefront of public thinking by modulating how much the president addressed them. This strategy did not seek to manufacture brand-new public policy preferences. Rather, its core mechanism was to use White House communications to trigger Americans to direct their attention to particular presidential positions and bolster personality traits.

Reflecting their realism, Nixon and Reagan tailored the content of their strategies to prime issues and images to independent real-world events and to the contours of public support for their existing policy positions and personality. For Nixon, his efforts at issue priming focused on domestic policy and on gaining public credit for his popular positions. He accentuated aggressive foreign policy to counteract sagging perceptions of him personally and, especially, his performance. Americans were preoccupied with the disliked Vietnam War, but he sought grudging respect for his character in seeking a workable path forward. He did not seek to warm the public's perceptions of him; instead, he accepted its evaluations and sought to accentuate its favorable impressions.

Reagan pursued priming strategies that navigated the particular realities of public opinion and real-world circumstances that faced him. Similarly to Nixon, he varied his priming efforts across policy domains. He primed popular domestic issues to claim credit among Americans. He sought to bolster perceptions of his leadership by accenting his economic policies while turning to diplomatic initiatives to project his personal warmth.

Presidents are, of course, not alone among political actors in pursuing priming strategies. They do, however, enjoy unique advantages through the White House's resources and unrivaled access to the media to laserbeam their messages to Americans. These advantages translate into what research on framing describes as message "strength" (namely, its credibility and likely resonance) and "competitive" edge when facing—as presidents normally do—rivals for the public's attention (Druckman 2011).

Sophisticated priming strategies contradict the presumption of commentators and students of political representation who assume that elites treat public opinion as a kind of sequestered jury, content to uncritically accept the public's priorities as unadulterated reflections of authentic

American attitudes. Presidential image priming points to an especially disturbing and potentially momentous pattern—the reconfiguring of political representation from a means for holding the substantive policy decisions of elected officials accountable. Instead, the efforts of political elites to track and then prime selected personality traits widen their discretion over policy and distance their decision making from the scrutiny and influence of the mass public. This strains the notion that the personal appeal of political figures is an idiosyncratic characteristic of unusually charismatic individuals (Shils 1965); presidential priming demonstrates the leveraging of White House institutions in an attempt to manufacture public perceptions of personality as a potential tool of manipulation.

This chapter tracked presidential strategies to change public opinion. The next chapter examines their effectiveness.

# PART III

# America's Democratic Dilemmas

### CHAPTER SIX

# The Effects and Limits of Presidential Efforts to Move Public Opinion

How effective are American government officials in influencing or manipulating public opinion to manufacture majority support for their agendas and policies? Successful manipulation, if proved true, guts a core democratic principle—citizens form authentic preferences that, in turn, drive government decisions (e.g., Bartels 2003; Disch 2011).[1]

The suspicion that political elites mold public opinion to fit their personal, short-term needs is long-standing. Since Thucydides's searing criticisms of Cleon in *The Peloponnesian War*, demagogues have been reviled for their skill in rallying the mass public through appeals to fear, ignorance, and prejudice. America's late eighteenth-century Constitution makers fretted about demagogues who sacrificed the broader public good by preying on "passions"[2] and on vanity through "obsequious court to the people."[3] The twentieth century and the rise of sophisticated mass communications intensified alarm at the potential of charismatic political figures—from Adolf Hitler to Joseph McCarthy—to exploit emotion to rally mass society (Gustainis 1990).

Where the fear of demagogues is rooted in distrust of the mass public and worries that it is vulnerable to emotional appeals, suspicions of powerful economic interests animate an alternative account of elite manipulation. According to Herman and Chomsky (1988), public opinion is generated by media coverage that conveys the perspectives and interests of owners and advertisers in order to satisfy the imperative of profitability. Social theorists and democratic theorists have argued that capitalism and its encompassing mass culture have short-circuited the formation of independent and critical attitudes, extinguishing meaningful reason-based public dialogue (Habermas 1989) and critical consciousness (Horkheimer and Adorno 1972). More recently, Disch (2011, 101) has concluded that elite scheming to craft the attitudes and perceptions of citizens renders them susceptible to "the possibility of . . . manipulation."

Disputes over the source of and threat to the possibility of authentic citizenship reflect debates and ambiguities regarding the meaning and scope of *manipulation* (Mansbridge 2003, 519). A full empirical analysis of manipulation would need to assess citizens' preferences against a counterfactual, but theorists and empirical scholars have failed thus far to agree on what that counterfactual should be (Druckman, in press). Another source of tension is the difficulty of making the distinction between elite persuasion or influence that is self-serving and efforts to move public opinion that are geared toward fostering education and civic learning. After all, John Kennedy and Lyndon Johnson pushed Americans to change their attitudes on civil rights in the 1960s when most opposed or were ambivalent toward the practical steps needed to achieve desegregation (Page and Shapiro 1992). A core conviction about the enduring public good tipped both presidents toward advocating civil rights as they faced powerful countervailing political pressures—responding to the demands of Democratic Party supporters versus placating the myriad southern white voters who would, eventually, embrace the Republican Party (Branch 1988, 1999; Jacobs and Shapiro 1994, 534). Kennedy's and Johnson's promotion of expanded civil rights (as they anticipated) mobilized support of as well as intense opposition to its implementation through busing, affirmative action, and other concrete policies. This turning point in American political development presents a daunting mix of constitutional and political debate over its effects, political expediency, and the ability of enlightened leadership to advance America's enduring values.

The conceptual complexity of manipulation is not an excuse, however, to abandon the concept altogether and lose the analytic capacity to pinpoint invidious efforts to move public opinion and distort public debate. As a general rule of thumb for present purposes, we associate manipulation with the calculated intent of elites to change public opinion for the sole or primary purpose of promoting their short-term and personal political interests, as opposed to advancing the enduring national interest (as evident in White House internal deliberations over civil rights).

Trepidations about the manipulative intent of political elites to advance themselves by forcing through consequential new policies are justified, as we have documented in previous chapters. Presidents since at least Lyndon Johnson have pursued a range of strategies to move public opinion and have changed their institutions to enhance their organizational capacity to manufacture mass support for their agenda and policies. Confidential records from White House files document, as we explore below, that these efforts extend beyond possibly benign efforts at education or more subtle forms of influence on the public's agenda of concerns to calibrated strategies to change public perceptions and attitudes to serve the White House's short-term political interests. This pattern of presidential intent to manipulate is not simply a quirk of personality that could be traced to Richard Nixon's paranoia or Lyndon Johnson's drive for domineering control; it endures across quite different types of presidents. Put simply, presidents have the incentives, administrative resources, and social learning to pursue concerted efforts to change public opinion to advance themselves and their policies.

But does the determined intent of political elites and presidents, in particular, to manipulate public opinion succeed? In this chapter, we address this question by focusing on a unique data set collected by Johnson. Specifically, we examine the gap between the president's intent to manipulate and the more limited effects of his efforts through a close study of his actions as the Vietnam War heated up. The Johnson White House makes a particularly compelling case study given the opportune conditions for successful elite manipulation: the administration was intensely motivated to shape public opinion; it invested more in polling than any previous administration to improve its effectiveness in moving public opinion and in aggressively applying the presidency's administrative machinery to achieving this objective; and it targeted not only domestic issues but also foreign policy, where Americans lack personal familiarity and their knowledge is imperfect (Jacobs and Shapiro 1995b; Rottinghaus 2010).

Our findings indicate that, under certain circumstances, Johnson was able to prime the public and in some cases even persuade Americans by moving their attitudes in a more manipulative fashion. Even this success, however, was quite uneven, particularly when it came to persuasion. In short, his influence was conditional and marginal compared to the sweeping expectations of the White House. This is not grounds for celebration given the threat to democracy, but it suggests that the White House's schemes routinely fall short of molding public opinion to its designs.

## Manipulation in Practice

Presidents largely attempt to move public opinion along two distinct dimensions. The first is through the process of priming that we discussed in the previous chapter—it is geared toward changing the emphasis that individuals place on the importance of a policy issue or personality trait. The second dimension is what we refer to as *manipulation*—persuading individuals to change their attitudes to support the particular policies favored by presidents even when real-world circumstances might reasonably lead to different conclusions. How did Johnson attempt to move public opinion, and what are reasonable expectations of his impacts?

### Johnson's Manipulative Intent

Presidents' public speeches often benefit from a presumption that their efforts educate the public about pressing problems and the need for action (Cohen 1995; Canes-Wrone 2006). The popular historian Doris Kearns Goodwin, for instance, pressed President Obama after the 2012 election to "use the bully pulpit to educate the country on the holistic approach [to gun control] . . . [by getting] out of the White House more . . . [to] talk to people about all of these issues."[4] Of course, few doubt that politics lurks behind presidential promotion, but many observers (like Kearns Goodwin) also welcome it as necessary to enlighten the public about the country's challenges and the menu of feasible options.

The beneficent assumption of presidential promotion collides with the reality of the modern presidency—the White House designs and initiates communications for the personal gain of the president. Conceptually attractive rationales for public education give way after inspection of archival records to a nearly opposite reality—the White House's single-minded orientation to incite public support in order to strengthen its influence over legislators and others.

The Johnson White House—like most of its successors—treated the public's attitudes as objects to be molded to fit its strategic needs. White House memoranda and reports reveal a two-pronged political strategy to expand Johnson's power—tracking public dissatisfaction for the purpose of priming what the public saw as important and persuading the public to prefer policy options favored by the administration. Johnson was a precursor to Nixon's and Reagan's use of priming that we examined in the previous chapter and engaged in a particularly sustained effort to both prime and, in some cases, persuade Americans to support his top policy initiatives—Vietnam and poverty reduction. Note that during Johnson's term in office (which we study) Vietnam was significantly lower than it would be later in terms of the public's view of the most important problem (hovering around 15 percent), and this prevented the ceiling effect encountered by Nixon when Vietnam became much more salient (in some periods over 40 percent).

DIAGNOSING SOURCES OF PUBLIC DISCONTENT: PRIMING VIA AGENDA SETTING. The first prong of the administration's strategy was diagnosis. The White House tracked the salience of and support for a range of foreign and domestic policies to identify the effect of Johnson's statements in building support for his agenda. More than any of its predecessors, it tracked opinion to measure and improve the effectiveness of the president's efforts to move opinion. During one period between September 1965 and September 1966, for instance, it received more than seventy polls from a variety of sources but mostly from its own pollster (Oliver Quayle). Reflecting the political importance of these polls, more than 90 percent were analyzed and sent along to the president's most senior staff (principally Bill Moyers), who generally forwarded them to the president (Jacobs and Shapiro 1995a; Jacobs and Burns 2004).

The White House aides turned to their ongoing polling to hone Johnson's rhetoric and, thus, set the public's agenda and affect what the public saw as important. The president's communications were, they calculated, a vehicle for priming. As a senior official put it, the administration's private polling was geared to "affect . . . the tone, the content, and the form of what we say publicly and privately."[5] Reflecting its commitment to shaping what the public focused on, the White House collected polling data on Americans' preferences and the importance that they attached to about six of ten issues that Johnson promoted publicly. By comparison, Nixon and Reagan collected these types of data on only 15 percent or less of the issues they addressed publicly. These Republican presidents shared their Democratic predecessor's aim to move public opinion, but they lacked his intense focus on shifting public attention from a devastating war.

The strategic corollary of presidential priming to elevate the importance of selected issues is its "crowding-out" effect. Elevating public concern about certain issues can displace attention to other issues that are especially damaging politically. Johnson deliberately made more public comments about pushing legislation through Congress to help the poor and create Medicare than about Vietnam in order to shift attention away from the politically damaging situation in Southeast Asia. The point was to move public opinion to "keep the President massively visible" and to "concentrate [media reporting] on the White House" in order to prime Americans to focus on favorable subjects and, thereby, prevent the "Vietnam War [from] dominat[ing] the headlines and the national mind."[6] As one aide warned, the White House faced "one-dimensional thinking" in which "the Vietnam War dominates the headlines and the national mind" and the administration's public standing and policy become threatened. Rather, he argued, "it is *essential* for the President to work harder to emphasize, as dramatically as possible, the more hopeful dimensions of America's face today."[7] Bill Moyers, a senior Johnson aide, eagerly flagged the White House's impact on public priorities in June 1966, pointing Johnson to polling data that the "rating of the War on Poverty is moving up in every state."[8]

As part of its strategy to change what Americans considered important and to refocus them on positively perceived topics, the White House mobilized officials and agencies throughout the executive branch. Capitalizing on the growing centralization of White House control (Moe 1985), Johnson's aides pressed the executive branch to "get across to the country the magnitude of what the Great Society has accomplished so far" and ensure that it was "properly be[ing] credited to the President in the public mind."[9]

MOVING PUBLIC OPINION: PERSUASION.    Johnson's second strategy was devoted to persuading the public to support administration policies. The administration's aggressive efforts to move public opinion were geared, as a Harvard academic (S. M. Lipset) recommended, toward "mak[ing] opinion [and] . . . not follow[ing] it."[10] Outsiders stressed the administration's "duty is to do what we [i.e., the administration] consider right . . . not what . . . 'the American people' want";[11] the calculus inside the White House was more complicated, blending debate over policy effectiveness with barebones calculations to mold the public to protect and advance its political position.

Johnson and his aides turned to the administration's "capacity to change the public mood" by identifying "What [Americans] now believe; What they may believe; and What they must be educated to believe."[12] The president's frequent public comments were treated as a weapon— according to voluminous archival records—to "handle volatile public opinion," to "change the public mood," and to "marshal[l] . . . American support for the Administration."[13] Revealing the strategic intent of White House communications, an aide hopefully reported to Johnson as the administration's public campaign expanded that "your agitation [and] your propaganda [are] finally softening up the opposition" and "reaching the American public in the way [the White House] wants them affected."[14]

The administration concentrated its campaign to change public opinion on two of its signature initiatives—Vietnam and the War on Poverty. A primary focus of the White House was to "persuad[e] people [that] we are making progress [in Vietnam]" and that they should change their preferences to support the administration's policies and, especially, its decision to expand US military commitments.[15] In addition, the administration pursued—according to previous research—a "massive rhetorical campaign" to develop support (Edwards 2009, 92).

What stood out about Johnson's efforts to move public opinion were his administration's efforts to improve effectiveness by using the White House's polls. One tool was to track trends to detect whether the president's activities were producing the desired change. The White House also relied on polls to pinpoint the most effective tactics. For instance, the administration polled to measure the impact of major presidential activities and speeches (such as the State of the Union address) on public attitudes and Johnson's approval ratings.[16] In addition, the White House used polls to pretest the president's appeals for public support in order to identify the most effective presentation. On Vietnam, for example, it targeted polling at exploring public reactions to the administration's position of fighting to force a negotiated peace that thwarted the Communist-controlled North.[17] This polling led to public presentations that framed the administration's Vietnam policy as a "middle-ground approach" to achieve an "honorable peace" through negotiations and judicious military force.

### The Prospects for Manipulating Presidents

What are the prospects for the president's intent to manipulate public opinion? The assumptions of presidents and political observers of a pliable public (e.g., Zaller 1992; Gabel and Scheve 2007; Bullock 2011) are contradicted by numerous studies that report that the White House's effect is, in general, marginal (Edwards 2009). Although presidents fall short of the sweeping impact they seek, they do have effects that are selective and conditional on prevailing political and real-world circumstances (Rottinghaus 2012).

PRESIDENTIAL WEAKNESS.    Much of the research specifically focused on presidential attempts to move public opinion reports marginal effects. Indeed, Edwards, who launched the "public presidency" field (see Edwards

1983), reports the persistent ineffectiveness of such attempts to manufacture public preferences or higher approval ratings (1996a, 1996b, 2003, 2007). Recent summaries of "minimal effects" research confirm that "evidence is mounting that presidents find difficulty in leading public opinion" (Tedin, Rottinghaus, and Rodgers 2011, 506) and that their "effectiveness [is] more problematic [than is often assumed]" (Cameron and Park 2011, 443).

Research on the causal chain of influence that the White House imagines—changed public opinion that converts congressional opposition into support—is even more negative. Presidents who rely on orchestrated appeals often find themselves with only marginal influence on lawmaking (Edwards 1989, 2007; Bond and Fleisher 1990) and victims of squandered political capital and frustrated public expectations (Baum 2004; Jerit 2008; Jacobs and Shapiro 2000). Presidents are unable to demonstrably move public opinion enough to register with legislators who have long-standing positions and commitments to constituents. The limited impact of presidential promotion saps the strategic utility of manipulation. In short, a substantial body of research refutes perceptions among elites by demonstrating that presidents have limited success at moving opinion.

SELECTIVE AND CONDITIONAL PRESIDENTIAL EFFECTS. Although the White House and others may exaggerate its capability to move public opinion, "writing off presidential leadership as totally ineffective" is also not warranted (Tedin, Rottinghaus, and Rodgers 2011, 506). Presidents exercise, we suggest, selective influences on public opinion that vary depending on prevailing political and real-world conditions (see also, e.g., Druckman and Holmes 2004; and Rottinghaus 2012; for a review, see Chong and Druckman 2012). Specifically, there are four circumstances that condition whether and to what extent the White House exerts influence.

First, individuals tend to interpret new arguments in light of their existing opinions: when people already hold strong opinions, they are prone to explicitly reject contrary arguments and are less likely to change their views (Visser, Bizer, and Krosnick 2006; Taber and Lodge 2006; Peffley and Hurwitz 2007). What this means is that the White House's effectiveness in tapping into *existing* public attitudes or identifying gaps in public knowledge creates particular opportunities for impact. Its administrative capacity to meticulously collect public opinion data equips it with the tools to hone its communications regarding issues on which Americans are susceptible to being moved. For example, Johnson's polling before 1966 revealed that Americans had not formed strong views about the Great Society's War on Poverty and the military war in Vietnam, spotlighting these issues in the eyes of the White House as vulnerable to promotional campaigns (Young 1991; Chafe 1986/2003).

Failure to anchor White House communications in existing public opinion runs the risk of colliding with well-formed attitudes and beliefs rooted in political party affiliation and interpersonal communications (Green, Palmquist, and Schickler 2002; Huckfeldt, Johnson, and Sprague 2004; Mutz 2006). Public opinion is not a blank slate that can somehow be manufactured or made out of thin air by elite manipulation. Elites can exercise influence, but the terms are set, in part, by the systematic processes by which individuals process information and construct preferences (Chong 1996; Price and Tewksbury 1997; Brewer 2001; Druckman 2001).

Second, competing messages from other elites and/or the media can neutralize presidential efforts to influence the public's opinions. By contrast, the absence of intense elite disagreement presents opportune circumstances for presidents to direct public opinion. This may be especially the case with foreign policy and war, where information may be secret, the public least informed, and the president most advantaged by his standing as the country's leader abroad and his unique control of national security information (Aldrich, Sullivan, and Borgida 1989; Holsti 2006; Berinsky 2009; Gelpi, Feaver, and Reifler 2009; Schudson 1995; Foyle 1999; Page and Shapiro 1992; Hill 1998, 1331). For Johnson, these conditions existed at the outset of the Vietnam War when Congress was united by anticommunism and voted nearly unanimously in favor of the Gulf of Tonkin Resolution in response to the purported attacks on US Navy vessels (Young 1991; Fisher 1995/2004).

Outside these unusually favorable circumstances for impact, however, presidents confront opponents and rivals with incentives to capitalize on their own positions of authority and access to the press to challenge White House presentations, which in turn is amplified by reporters and editors (Jacobs and Shapiro 2000, 2011; Chong and Druckman 2007, 2010). Research shows that counterframes often offset each other and that negative counterframes of the sort typically introduced in response to presidential messages are particularly potent in motivating individuals to resist any one perspective (Druckman 2004). For example, President George W. Bush's presentation of the Iraq War as necessary to protect American security was persistently and effectively countered by counterframes that emphasized the grim reality on the ground and the costs to America (Baum and Groeling 2010).

Third, the president's own history sets parameters on what can be done. Presidents with checkered histories on an issue or low credibility face constraints (Druckman and Lupia 2000; Chong and Druckman 2007). Presidents with strong approval ratings are more successful in shaping public opinion, while unpopular presidents are less effective (Page, Shapiro, and Dempsey 1987; Page and Shapiro 1984; but cf. Cohen 1995). In the year after his 1964 landslide election, Johnson was quite popular—peaking at above 70 percent and averaging 66 percent during 1965—and enjoyed more impact on Americans. When his approval sharply declined to 50 percent in 1966, the conditions for moving public opinion worsened.

Fourth, efforts by elites to direct public opinion are colored by real-world events, especially if circumstances and communications clash. Accurate information about events—such as wartime casualties or the end of the Cold War—can shift attitudes (Page and Shapiro 1992). Efforts by President Johnson to build support for his Vietnam policies by proclaiming their effectiveness depended on favorable events on the ground; the Vietcong's Tet Offensive in January 1968 failed militarily but hurt Johnson because his public message of progress was undercut by evidence of vulnerability and the need for substantial and costly sustained US commitments (Berman 1989; Schandler 1977; Wirtz 1991).

Our synthesis of existing research suggests that the Johnson White House's sweeping plans to "change the public mood" and to "marshal[l] . . . American support for the Administration" are *unlikely to succeed in general*.[18] There are, however, selective opportunities for elites to affect public opinion through priming and persuasion.

Priming is the more promising mechanism for moving public opinion because citizens tend to have less crystalized views on what is important and there is less debate about it (relative to views on specific issues). As Cohen (1995, 102) explains: "The president does not have to convince the public that a policy problem is important by offering substantive positions. Merely mentioning a problem to the public heightens public concern with the policy problem" (see also Druckman and Holmes 2004). The public need not agree with the president's position or be persuaded by it; it simply must appreciate that the problem is important, and the president mentioning it may increase attention to it. For Johnson, however, his opportunities to prime public opinion varied across policy domains. On the domestic front, he had substantial leeway to prime, especially on his novel hallmark initiative—the War on Poverty—which was new to the public. By contrast, Vietnam already registered as important in the minds of Americans owing to real-world events and the administration's policies. Although this complicated his priming efforts, Johnson enjoyed credibility on foreign policy (until late in his term) as well as the ability to exert some control over what national security information became public (Page and Shapiro 1992; Foyle 1999; Hill 1998, 1331).

Our expectation, then, is that Johnson's effort to prime should generally succeed, in general, in elevating the importance of foreign policy issues and his antipoverty initiative.

Persuasion poses stiffer hurdles for elites intent on moving public opinion because the public's preferences regarding policy are held more strongly and stubbornly; we see it as more akin to manipulation (see chapter 1). On Vietnam, the public was susceptible to influence during the war's early stage prior to 1966 when majorities approved of Johnson's job performance, which, as we have seen, rose above 70 percent in early 1965. With that support, the public, the media, and members of Congress backed him during the 1964 Gulf of Tonkin incident and the 1965 Viet Cong attack on a US airbase (Rottinghaus 2010, 137–41). Persuasion became more daunting after 1965, however, as policy preferences for and against the administration's approach strengthened and crystallized and elites divided. On domestic issues and, specifically, his antipoverty initiative, Johnson enjoyed greater opportunities to persuade Americans to adopt his position because they had not yet adopted strong views.

In short, our integration of previous research and presidential strategy suggests that selective circumstances—unformed public attitudes and elite comity—generated openings for Johnson to prime Americans on foreign affairs and antipoverty policy and to persuade them on poverty and Vietnam before 1966. Beyond these situations, however, we expect the president to make little headway driving public opinion despite the White House's massive efforts and ambitious plans.

## Presidential Effects

### Studying Johnson's Effects on Americans

Our data for quantitatively analyzing Johnson's effects on public opinion come from our unique collection of privately conducted polls assembled by the White House. Although later presidents would expand the scope of their polling, Johnson tracked a smaller set of issues, which we group in twelve key policy areas: seven are in domestic affairs (government spending, antipoverty initiatives, broader social welfare entitlements, government reform, business incentives, expanding civil rights, and social conservatism), and five are in foreign policy (foreign aid and imports, relations with allies, prevailing in Vietnam, fighting communism, and keeping the peace). The first column of table 6.1 contains our list of twelve issues, while the second lists the domain.

As in previous chapters, we converted these variables of public opinion and presidential statements into monthly measures. Our analysis focuses on the thirty-seven months from December 1963 through December 1966, creating a maximum number of 432 observations.[19] In practice, the number of observations for the White House's public opinion data reported in table 6.1 is lower because the White House did not collect data on all issues in every month.

Our first dependent variable, which measures priming, is *importance*. Johnson measured it in White House polls as the percentage of Americans who identified particular issues as important. This survey item provided respondents with a list of issues and asked them to identify those that were "most important" (multiple responses were recorded). Not surprisingly, Vietnam was by far the public's greatest concern, followed by poverty, whose ranking was nearly half of Vietnam's (29 vs. 17.5 percent). Did Johnson's statement lead respondents in White House polls to change what they saw as important? If they did, under what conditions did his influence register?

Our second measure is the public's policy preferences—the percentage supporting "keeping the peace" or "helping the poor," for example. The *directional support score* measure makes it possible to study the impact of Johnson's effort at persuasion. Did his public statements affect the public's support for his policies to reduce poverty and to conduct the war in Vietnam? What conditions most favored his efforts?

We created three independent variables to measure the conditions under which we expect Johnson to influence public opinion. The most significant is his public statements. For our analysis of priming, we constructed a measure of *emphasis* by counting the number of times per month the president mentioned a particular issue in his public statements in the prior month. If he did not make a statement on a given issue in a given month, we coded it as a 0 since he opted to ignore the issue.

For our persuasion analyses, we created a measure of *directional policy position* on particular issues by coding the directionality of Johnson's public statements according to a five-point scale ranging from –2 (oppose

TABLE 6.1 **Issues, Positions, Average Scores**

| Area | Domain | Example Positions. | Average Support for Issue Position (SD; N) | Average Importance (SD; N) | Average Weighted Johnson's Position (SD; N) | Average Johnson's Mentions (SD; N) |
|---|---|---|---|---|---|---|
| Foreign aid/imports | Foreign | Favor cutting imports; favor isolationism | 46.87 (7.43; 28) | 5.13 (2.55; 28) | -6.84 (13.20; 36) | 1.76 (2.10; 37) |
| Relations with allies | Foreign | Support better relations with South America; support improved US-French relations | 46.07 (10.93; 28) | 6.09 (2.91; 30) | 23.85 (30.74; 36) | 4.46 (5.17; 37) |
| Vietnam | Foreign | Support commitment to Vietnam | 41.16 (12.60; 31) | 29.24 (17.89; 27) | 98.55 (81.16; 36) | 9.16 (6.85; 37) |
| Communism | Foreign | Support challenging Russia; support end of colonial rule | 55.91 (7.45; 28) | 12.28 (6.40; 28) | 12.93 (22.15; 36) | 6.41 (13.03; 37) |
| Peace | Foreign | Favor the UN; support limiting arms testing | 69.58 (9.17; 28) | 8.54 (3.56; 28) | 21.57 (57.96; 36) | 4.84 (6.59; 37) |
| Spending | Domestic | Support cutting welfare; support cutting taxes | 39.98 (13.54; 28) | 12.90 (6.12; 28) | 20.29 (36.81; 36) | 5.95 (7.32; 37) |
| Poor, workers | Domestic | Support War on Poverty (i.e., antipoverty); support increase to the minimum wage | 53.71 (12.78; 34) | 17.48 (5.62; 30) | 22.54 (29.13; 36) | 15.27 (21.86; 37) |

TABLE 6.1 (*continued*)

| Area | Domain | Example Positions | Average Support for Issue Position (SD; *N*) | Average Importance (SD; *N*) | Average Weighted Johnson's Position (SD; *N*) | Average Johnson's Mentions (SD; *N*) |
|---|---|---|---|---|---|---|
| Entitlements | Domestic | Support expansion of Social Security; support more medical care for aged | 60.15 (7.84; 28) | 15.35 (5.75; 30) | 28.00 (41.98; 36) | 12.60 (23.35; 37) |
| Government reform | Domestic | Support reform of mail service; support reform of banking system | Not asked | 4.10 (2.13; 5) | 8.06 (13.39; 36) | 2.43 (2.75; 37) |
| Business | Domestic | Support stimulation of private investment | Not asked | 5.10 (2.81; 7) | 16.06 (37.05; 36) | 2.32 (4.28; 37) |
| Civil rights | Domestic | Support improving race relations | 45.21 (14.09; 28) | 14.46 (9.47; 28) | 67.46 (111.62; 36) | 4.22 (5.80; 37) |
| Social conservatism | Domestic | Favor gun control; support separation of church/state | Not asked | 7.88 (3.32; 7) | −6.82 (17.92; 36) | 1.54 (2.46; 37) |
| Total | | | 50.91 (14.15; 261) | 12.90 (10.15; 276) | 25.47 (56.95; 432) | 5.91 (11.58; 432) |

issue) to 2 (support it), with 0 indicating neutrality. The directionality of Johnson's positions was weighted by space—the number of lines devoted to talking about a particular policy in his public statements. Note that we did not put this on a standardized 0–1 scale since we weighted by space, making it theoretically not finite; we weighted in this case because of evidence that, when it comes to public opinion, repetition can have significant effects (see Zaller 1992; Fernandes 2013).[20] (The direction of Johnson's position as we coded it is in the third column of table 6.1.) This is consistent with the expectation from the Johnson White House and considerable academic research that strong, repeated *positions* improve elite impact as individuals are more exposed to a clearly communicated message (e.g., Claibourn 2008). For both the importance and the directional data, we used White House polling that was collected at regular intervals in order to gauge impact.

In general, we use a one-month lag of the presidential statement; Johnson's effect can register only after his statement has been made and has been covered by the media. If no statement was made in the prior month, we do *not* use the most recently available presidential statement (as in other chapters) because the public is not likely to recall presidential comments from long ago when asked for its opinions. Substantial evidence suggests that political communication effects are short-lived (Chong and Druckman 2010; Gerber, Gimpel, Green, and Shaw 2011). We also include the lagged values of the dependent variables (the public's support for issue areas and the importance it attached to them one month earlier than Johnson's statements); we model these as a third independent variable in our overall analyses. The lagged dependent variable serves as a control to detect Johnson's impact on citizen attitudes apart from the inertial qualities of public opinion, which we identified earlier as an important constraint on presidential influence.[21] This poses a stringent test of Johnson's effect: Is he able to change the public's agenda and policy preferences from their starting points in the previous month?

Table 6.1 provides details on average support, importance, Johnson's positions, and mentions for each issue that reveal several strategic opportunities and constraints facing the White House. The president's calibration of White House polling to aid his efforts to move public opinion is reflected in his tendency to collect importance data and directional policy data much more frequently than did Nixon or Reagan: Johnson collected importance data 62 percent (276/444) of the time, compared to 7 percent for Nixon and 15 percent for Reagan; he collected directional policy data

58 percent (261/444) of the time, compared to 7 percent for Nixon and 4.5 percent for Reagan. In addition, table 6.1 shows the White House's calibration of the president's statements in the wide variance in the monthly measures of weighted position; this stems largely from Johnson's shifting of emphasis from month to month rather than radically shifting his own position. These shifts are also apparent in the notable variance in the mention data. Another revealing aspect of table 6.1 is what it tells us about the well-formed public opinion that confronted Johnson's efforts to prime and persuade Americans: keeping the peace registered the maximum support, and Vietnam received the strongest ratings for importance (29 percent of the public scored it most important); expanding entitlements and helping the poor received strong public support (poverty received the second highest importance rating at 17.5 percent).

### Johnson's Selective and Conditional Effects

Johnson failed to manipulate public opinion to suit his sweeping political objectives—to dictate what issues Americans considered important and to manufacture their support for his policies. Although its efforts fell short of his intentions, the White House did exert an impact on public opinion—but one that was selective and conditional.

CONSTRAINED PRIMING.   We explore the success of the White House's priming strategy to elevate the public's attention to advantageous issues and to diminish the importance attached to Vietnam, especially as the war became unpopular. We test for priming by regressing the public's importance score on the Johnson's emphasis variable (from the prior month) and the lagged dependent variable, which, as explained, allows us to control for inertia in public opinion and ensures that any impact we find reflects the president actually moving people's opinions.[22] Table 6.2 displays regression results for Johnson's priming efforts on four sets of policy domains: (a) all issues, (b) domestic only, (c) foreign only, and (d) poverty only.

Johnson's effectiveness in priming varied by policy domain and the distinctive conditions each presented. Table 6.2 shows that, across all issues, the president's statements did prime importance—when he emphasized an issue, the public followed suit. The magnitude of this effect, however, is marginal (but not meaningless): across all issues, Johnson's mentioning of a policy had a .12 effect on the public's ranking of that policy. Substan-

TABLE 6.2 **Impact of Johnson's Statements on Public Importance (Dependent Variable: Public Importance)**

|                      | All Issues | Domestic | Foreign | Antipoverty Only |
| -------------------- | ---------- | -------- | ------- | ---------------- |
| Johnson's emphasis   | .12**      | .10**    | .21**   | .10**            |
|                      | (.04)      | (.03)    | (.06)   | (.03)            |
| Importance, $t-1$    | .78**      | .41**    | .88**   | .28              |
|                      | (.03)      | (.08)    | (.04)   | (.19)            |
| Constant             | 2.57**     | 7.89**   | .74     | 11.43**          |
|                      | (.68)      | (1.25)   | (.79)   | (3.50)           |
| $R^2$                | .64        | .26      | .80     | .24              |
| $N$                  | 233        | 113      | 120     | 26               |

*Note*: The table reports OLS coefficients with standard errors in parentheses. ** $p \leq .05$, * $p \leq .10$, one-tailed test.

tively, he would have to mention it ten times to contribute to a 1 percent increase in importance.

What stands out in table 6.2, however, is Johnson's particular impact on foreign policy, as we predicted. The president's impact is significantly greater on foreign affairs (coefficient of .21) than on domestic affairs (coefficient of .10). While we did not predict a significant impact on domestic policy, his promotion of antipoverty and the War on Poverty accounts for this effect: the last column in table 6.2 shows that, when we look *only* at the poverty issue, his statements did somewhat move public opinion (.10), but not to the extent we expected. In short, his promotion of policies to reduce poverty did increase the public's sense of the importance of the issue but failed to elevate attention to it as substantially as the White House schemed. When we remove the issue from our domestic regression in table 6.2, Johnson's statements fall to insignificance (analysis not displayed). This further confirms our earlier expectation that Johnson would be able to prime his War on Poverty.

Johnson's success in priming was contingent on certain conditions, as we suggested earlier. Among all issues, the public's prior ratings of importance exert large and statistically significant effects. The one exception reinforces our general argument about contingency and real-world circumstances: the effect of Johnson on the public's ranking of antipoverty as important is not huge but mattered more than what the public had thought just one month earlier. This shows the leeway that presidents enjoy on novel programs that lack well-formed public attitudes.

One of the most striking failures of the White House's priming strategy was the effort to distract the public from the souring situation in Vietnam. While our foreign affairs regression in table 6.2 supports our prediction of priming in general, Johnson was unable to prevent Vietnam from "dominat[ing] public thinking"—as one staffer put it—by focusing the public on more favorably perceived issues.[23] (The effect in table 6.2 is driven by non-Vietnam foreign affairs issues.) *When we limit our foreign affairs regression only to Vietnam*, Johnson's statements had no statistically significant effect (analysis not shown).[24] When we exclude Vietnam from our foreign affairs regression, Johnson's influence grows a bit to a significant coefficient of .23. In other words, the president was able to prime foreign affairs, but he was not able to dislodge Vietnam as a most important problem in the eyes of Americans. The souring circumstances on the ground in Vietnam and the media's reporting of them prevented him from influencing the public's perception of the issue's importance. The public persistently rated Vietnam as extremely important, regardless of what Johnson had to say. This contradicts one of the White House's central strategic objectives and assumptions about its capacity to move public opinion.

In contrast to the expectations from past research, Johnson's public approval had limited effects on his ability to prime. High approval ratings (which Johnson enjoyed prior to 1966) did not reliably translate into unprecedented presidential influence on the public's ranking of issue importance in the realms of domestic and foreign affairs.[25]

Overall, Johnson's effects were selective and conditional, falling far short of the White House's ambitions to control the public's agenda to activate advantageous considerations as it evaluated the president and his policies. Johnson was able to prime the War on Poverty and foreign affairs but no other issues.

MARGINAL PERSUASION.    Our test for persuasion follows our approach to priming: we regress the public's issue positions on Johnson's weighted issue positions and the public's positions lagged one time period. (The issue positions are in the same direction as listed in table 6.1 above.) As with priming, we begin with the basic persuasion model for all data and then test separately for domestic and foreign. The results are presented in table 6.3.

Johnson's effectiveness in persuading Americans is quite mixed, following the pattern of selectivity and conditionality. In contrast to his priming effects across all issues, the president had no persuasive influence: the first column in table 6.3 shows that prior support levels had a large impact (.70) but that his statement had *no* significant effect on the public's issue positions. Johnson was, however, successful at persuasion in the domain

TABLE 6.3 **Impact of Johnson's Statements on Directional Support (Dependent Variable: Directional Support)**

| | All Issues | Domestic | Foreign | Antipoverty Only | Vietnam Prior to 1966 |
|---|---|---|---|---|---|
| Johnson's directional | .01 | .04** | −.002 | .19** | .09** |
| statement | (.01) | (.02) | (.06) | (.06) | (.02) |
| Positions, $t-1$ | .70** | .63** | .76** | .56** | .64** |
| | (.05) | (.08) | (.06) | (.13) | (.11) |
| Constant | 14.84** | 17.69** | 12.09** | 20.00** | 3.85 |
| | (2.69) | (4.12) | (3.49) | | (4.53) |
| $R^2$ | .48 | .42 | .56 | .55 | .96 |
| $N$ | 217 | 100 | 117 | 31 | 9 |

*Note*: The table reports OLS coefficients with standard errors in parentheses. ** $p \le .05$, * $p \le .10$, one-tailed test.

of domestic affairs but not foreign. (The lagged support continues to be significant.) As we predicted, the president's persuasive effect on domestic affairs came strictly from the War on Poverty program, as shown in the fourth regression. If his statements on attacking poverty reached their average weighted score, then public support would rise about 4 percent—a significant effect in both statistical and substantive terms.[26] This general finding is confirmed by separate analyses (not reported in the table) that detect a statistically significant interaction of Johnson's statements on poverty reduction and the public's support of the issue (i.e., an interaction with the poverty issue and Johnson's statements). Further confirming the selective nature of his persuasion, the president had no effect on domestic affairs overall or individual policy areas when we *excluded* the War on Poverty (not shown). Although these findings confirm our expectations, they do contradict the common assumption that the public is more susceptible to elite influence on foreign affairs because presidents control information and regularly assert unilateral power to act, often in secret (Aldrich, Sullivan, and Borgida 1989; Page and Shapiro 1992).

Johnson failed to persuade Americans to adopt his foreign policy positions overall, but he did secure—as we predicted—selected success on Vietnam in the year after his election. When we look *only* at Vietnam prior to 1966, he exerted a notably sized effect on the public's policy opinions—he produced an average 10 percent increase. This is consistent with some past research, including Rottinghaus's (2010, 140) report that "the public followed the president's lead on the administration's new course of action in Vietnam" (see also Edwards 2003, 91; and Jacobs and Shapiro 1999).

The conditional nature of Johnson's persuasion suggests the limits of his influence. His influence on the public's position on Vietnam quickly disappeared (in 1966) as opinions crystallized. His efforts to persuade Americans in 1966 were overtaken by the souring conditions in Southeast Asia and by the public's backlash against Johnson, which contributed to sweeping Republican wins in the 1966 elections.

In the end, Johnson's persuasive effect was limited to one year, one domestic program, and one foreign affairs issue—under unusually advantageous conditions. Even determined presidential efforts to change the public's policy preferences are constrained by existing attitudes and real-world circumstances.

## Strategic Elites and Adaptive Publics

The high expectations of the White House (and some scholars) of its ability to move public opinion fall far short of President Johnson's actual (marginal and contingent) impact on the public's concerns and policy preferences. The study of presidents teaches a healthy appreciation for the distinction between presidential strategic intent to move public opinion and the actual effect of the White House on Americans. The president's motivations, administrative resources, and social learning in how to mold public opinion reveal an apparently unrelenting devotion to self-serving manipulation. Although the distinction between elite efforts to manipulate and elite efforts to educate for the public good has been difficult to disentangle in the abstract (Mansbridge 2003, 519), this and earlier chapters reveal an unmistakable reality—presidents from different parties, historical periods, and circumstances have routinely attempted to move public opinion to advance their short-term political interests.

The White House's ambitious and administratively sophisticated efforts to move public opinion have not, however, produced the sweeping changes imagined within the sanctum of the Oval Office. This chapter's investigation of Johnson found that he was able to prime the public to change the importance it attaches to particular issues (especially poverty reduction and foreign affairs). But these effects were selective and conditional. Revealing still greater vulnerability, his attempts to persuade Americans to support his policy positions delivered even fewer results; these are limited to the novel War on Poverty and Vietnam in its early stages.

Although Johnson did exercise selective influence, the overall thrust of the findings from our analysis is closer to a broad pattern of marginal effects (Edwards 2003, 2007). Soon after his inauguration in 1981, Ronald Reagan aggressively attempted to build public support for converting Social Security into a voluntary program but found (according to his own private polling) that he had failed to deliver converts and was actually undermining support for his presidency among key groups of voters (Jacobs 2005, 2011). Conceding the limits on his promotional powers, he flipped directions from attempting to dismantle Social Security as a compulsory program that covered nearly all Americans to building a bipartisan coalition in 1983 that strengthened the program's finances for decades to come. Bill Clinton's elaborate effort a decade later to sell his "managed-competition" approach to health care reform in 1993–1994 provided an impressive display of the presidency's communications arsenal but ended similarly with failure—a majority of Americans came to oppose it (Jacobs and Shapiro 2000). George W. Bush's efforts following his 2004 reelection to rally the public behind partially privatizing Social Security reached the same end point—failure and rising public opposition (Jacobs 2010).

Given the uneven or perhaps dismal record of White House promotions, why do presidents invest in them? Weakness and the search for even contingent means to expand their scarce political resources is a consideration. In addition, the White House's evolving administrative capacity and social learning about how to attempt to move public opinion may inflate its confidence. After being elected to carry out an ambitious mandate, presidents face constitutional and institutional quicksand that makes the unsteady branch of public promotion appear attractive and worthy of investment.

What are the implications of White House campaigns to move public opinion? First, presidential promotions are constrained, but they do exert targeted impacts under certain circumstances that raise sobering normative concerns about the authenticity of public opinion. Are government policies responding to semisovereign citizen preferences or to powerful elites who hold sway over public opinion?

Second, inflated White House expectations impose costs: staking out positions that exceed what is feasible can squander opportunities or produce blunders, as in the case of Vietnam. Johnson's confidence that he could build and sustain public support for his policy in Southeast Asia by withholding or distorting information (as the Pentagon Papers reveal) led him to expand the commitment of US troops from about 15,000 under John Kennedy to over 500,000 and to unleash a massive air bombardment that would eventually amount to four times the tonnage used during all of World War II (Young 1991; Chafe 1986/2003).

White House polling analysts cheered on Johnson's swelling commitments with a steady stream of upbeat reports of public support while persistently downplaying evidence of growing doubt and stubborn opposition.[27] Typical of the administration's excessive confidence in controlling
public opinion, a White House aide assured the president in December
1965 that Americans "supported the military increases made during the
past year . . . [and] in some respects would be willing to go further . . . because they think it will bring a peaceful solution nearer."[28] White House
reports in 1966 continued to find "a great deal of support" for the president's policy of "keep[ing] military pressure on but seek[ing] a negotiated settlement."[29] Indeed, only days before the politically devastating Tet
Offensive in 1968, a White House official enthusiastically reported that
the public's approval of the president had soared and that "Vietnam is
well in hand" because "the public has greater understanding of what the
administration is trying to do in Vietnam."[30] Tet's contradiction of the administration's public assurances of progress precipitated a drop in public
support and a new (belated) realism in the White House: as one official
put it in March 1968, "I don't think anything we can say about the war will
transcend the events on the ground."[31] Johnson agreed and on March 31,
1968, withdrew from the presidential race and his potential campaign for
reelection, accepting that his objectives in Vietnam were not obtainable
and could no longer attract public backing (Ripley 1993).

While Johnson's efforts to mold public opinion may be exceptional, his
experience underscores the potentially high costs of relying on inflated
expectations of presidential promotions—costs incurred from commit-
ting to an unsustainable agenda that precipitates public backlash. Indeed,
these sobering consequences were absorbed after Reagan's and Bush's
drives to privatize Social Security and Clinton's crusade to transform
health care following the 1992 election failed to give him a clear mandate
and left his party short of adequate congressional majorities.

Sweeping conclusions about the impact of elites both inflate beyond
recognition the impact of elites and miss the more subtle but potentially
significant influences that elites do exercise. Serious appraisal of presidents' efforts to shape public opinion needs to focus on revealing their
pervasive institutionalized intent while narrowing (rather than enlarging)
the range of their actual influence.

### CHAPTER SEVEN

# Rethinking Representation

The practice of political representation has eclipsed classic theories about Western democracy. Generations of political theorists and scholars of American politics assumed that representation is a one-way relationship in which the public's preferences regarding policies are studied for their effects on government decision making. The democratic theorist Bryan Garsten (2009, 90) observes: "Most of the political science literature simply presumes that the purpose of representative government is to be an instrument of the popular will" (see also Shapiro 2011).

The one-way conception of representation has been undercut by our research findings that question the basic framework of presumed responsiveness. In the past, theorists and empirical researchers have concentrated on the *policy preferences* of the general public, but the reality is that elites widen their latitude on policy by largely ignoring the views of citizens on issues that are not salient, by priming what issues are salient, and by triggering the public to evaluate them on their *perceived personality* rather than on policy issues (as documented in chapters 3–5). Even as the scope of representation narrows, conventional analysis of political representation assumes that government officials treat each citizen equally as a generic "median voter," but the reality is that political elites are mostly concerned with the demands of particular, privileged segments of the electorate that are affluent, well organized, and/or politically valued (as shown in chapter 4). All these patterns sharply depart from classic democratic theory, but that is not all. Government officials view and treat public opinion as a malleable object to be molded to support them and their policies, flipping the one-way presumption of the responsiveness account on its head. Weaving together these strands of American politics points to a system of governance that diminishes or obstructs democratic responsiveness.

Has American democracy been grievously wounded as representation has become narrowed, segmented, and threatened by elite efforts to move public opinion? Not necessarily. Elite strategies often fail (as shown in chapter 6). Elections and other forms of political participation as well as institutionalized influence may remain potent under certain conditions, generating pressure for translating sustained, strong public preferences into government policy. The challenge is to develop a framework for understanding representation that both acknowledges the barriers to democracy in contemporary American politics and remains attuned to opportunities to leverage elite competition and citizen mobilization in an environment in which power and its resources remain sufficiently scattered, under certain circumstances, to permit meaningful conflict and some degree of democratic attentiveness. America can best be understood as a form of *neopolyarchy*—a modification of Robert Dahl's (1971) notion of representation. Dahl skillfully spotlighted the conditions of elite competition and its effects—on checking the dominance of any single faction and elevating receptivity to enduring public concerns. Harvesting the conceptual value of polyarchy requires, however, scrutiny of its overly optimistic assumptions that formal rights and fair procedures would generate citizens' "wishes" based on their own interests (as opposed to citizens' views generated by elite priming and other strategies) and "elections [that] hold political leaders accountable to [voters]" (Prewett 1970, 5). We integrate Dahl's nuanced analysis of elite competition with a more realistic appreciation of the limits of representation and the importance of mobilizing citizens into political arenas—lifting their awareness of their stakes and generating opportunities for revitalizing citizenship and participation.

This chapter begins by synthesizing the findings of our book and previous research with the core dilemmas of democratic representation. The second section turns to outlining a model of representation that attends to both the frailties of American representation and the opportunities for strengthening it.

## The Narrowing of Democracy

Three core questions animate debates about American democracy: What, who, and how do elites engage in representation in practice? We address these questions by marshaling the evidence that we have presented in previous chapters along with large bodies of research.

*What Is Represented?*

Chapters 2 and 3 reveal that modern presidents expanded their institutional capacity to collect and analyze public polling data (much of it privately commissioned) in order to widen their leeway. They do this by catering to their most valued supporters while winning over swing voters necessary to secure reelection for themselves and their allies. We found that strategic calculations and political circumstances led Nixon and Reagan to alternate between a lumping approach of tracking general ideological dispositions and a more costly splitting approach of detecting attitudes toward individual issues. Their investment of the time and resources to collect information on specific issues was tied to the public's prioritizing of national problems of importance and to the risk of mishandling them: absent public scrutiny and the risk of damaging punishment as elections approached, White House strategists economized scarce resources by relying on lumping. Distinct political circumstances further refined each president's approach to which type of public information to collect and use. Reagan relied on his polling to accommodate conservatives until he risked alienating swing voters (as in the case of his unveiling and then rejection of his proposal to make Social Security voluntary). Nixon took the more opportunistic approach of using his polling to pinpoint openings of voter disinterest to stake out conservative positions that quieted his restless base.

In addition, Nixon and Reagan widened the scope of White House polling from collecting information on the public's policy preferences. They devoted more resources to tracking the image of presidents and, specifically, closely monitoring the public's evaluations of their personality traits.

Our excavation and quantitative analyses of the polling operations of Nixon and Reagan reveal two critical aspects of political representation that would not be apparent from empirical research and classic democratic theory adopting the one-way conception of representation. First, empirical research that relies on publicly available polling data operates on the false assumption that presidents use their private information similarly to the way in which scholars use published data. Breaking into the black box of White House decision making demonstrates that presidents act as strategic gatherers of information rather than relying on arbitrarily assembled data. The political logic of presidential collection and use of particular types of polling information is tied to strategic circumstances and the risk of voter scrutiny and punishment—the proximity of elections,

first cut about representation but fail to control for confounding factors such as the disproportionate attention to the affluent and well-organized (Jacobs and Page 2005) or the possibility that public opinion has been primed to focus on issues of importance to political elites, as our previous chapters demonstrate. Our integration of archival and quantitative research offers a unique approach for investigating political representation that is both rigorous and grounded.

## Who Is Represented?

Chapter 4 found evidence that presidents—Reagan, in particular—were highly attentive to the demands of privileged segments of the electorate with high incomes and other politically valued resources. Our analyses of the inside machinations piece together the microfoundations of segmented representation at a critical juncture when the New Deal coalition had unraveled but a durable, winning alternative coalition had yet to form. Archival records and quantitative analyses show Reagan's creation of a New Right coalition that recruited social conservatives to the old base of Republicans and military and fiscal conservatives. The glue for this coalition building was adopting entirely new positions favored by evangelicals (i.e., born-again Protestants) and catering to the interests of the affluent in scaling back taxes and government social programs while playing to GOP hawks.

Our investigation of Reagan's behind-the-scenes strategizing fills out a growing body of aggregate-level analyses documenting the influence of organized interests on government policy. Beginning with the pioneering research of Miller and Stokes (1963), empirical studies of political representation focused on the close congruence of public opinion and government policy. The study of congruence and responsiveness failed, however, to appreciate the multiple and competing forms of representation (Pitkin 1967; Mansbridge 2003, 2011; Rehfeld 2006) and the segmentation of government responsiveness. Bartels (2008), Gilens (2005, 2012), and others report consistent evidence that members of Congress attend to the preferences of the affluent more than less-well-off citizens. Wood (2009) shows the disproportionate impact of the president's base of support on his administration. Jacobs and Page (2005) show that the simple but strong bivariate relationship between public opinion and policy disappears after including the omitted variable of corporate interests, which exerts the strongest effects. Hacker and Pierson (2010) trace the growing affluence of the superrich—the top 1 percent—and their rising political muscle flexed through organized groups and the political parties to effect changes in taxes, spending, regulations, and labor relations that favor their interests at the expense of most Americans. The general thrust of these studies of contemporary American politics is consistent with our findings about Reagan; our contribution is to use analysis of often-confidential archival records to break into the black box of political calculations to explain aggregate patterns detected by other scholars and reveal the array of interests (from the affluent to evangelicals, in Reagan's case) that are considered politically valuable. Studying representation from within the Oval Office makes it possible to stitch together the disparate shards of political calculations, presidential actions, and polling data into a portrait of why and how representation is biased toward the better off.

In sum, one of the implications of our findings and those of prior researchers is that we should question the self-serving proclamations of presidents that they are "stewards of the people" who serve the entire country and its greater good (Gerring 1998; Bimes and Mulroy 2004). The reality vividly captured by our inside-the-black-box vantage point demonstrates that presidents pay more attention to the better organized and established than to everyday citizens. Private White House polling that might on the surface appear to confirm responsiveness to the general public is used for quite different purposes—to cater to narrow interests and mobilize new political constituencies.

### Do Politicians Treat Citizens as Their Principals?

Labor relations and bureaucratic politics have been explained by economists and positive theorists as structured by the relationship between the principal, who enjoys the authority associated with elevated hierarchical position, and the agent, who is in a subordinate position and, thus, compelled to comply. The principal-agent model has been used to account for the control of lawmakers over the unelected bureaucracy (McCubbins, Noll, and Weingast 1987, 1989; Moe 1987; Miller 2005). It also has been applied to democratic accountability and the expectation that voters act as principals to sanction wayward politicians and select candidates with favored traits and positions (Fearon 1999). Although the principal-agent theory is elegant in its formulation, its application to democratic accountability rests on a faulty foundational assumption—that elected officials treat voters as their principals.

Our combination of archival and quantitative research on inner White House strategizing reveals that the president and his senior aides treat voters not as principals to be followed but as targets to be molded to their designs. Chapter 5 documents the calibrated strategies of Nixon and Reagan to prime Americans to direct their attention to popular presidential positions and to bolster selected personality traits. Nixon focused on gaining public credit for his popular domestic positions and accentuating his aggressive foreign policies (such as his handling of Vietnam) to counteract sagging perceptions of him personally. Reagan too primed popular domestic issues to claim credit but adapted to different political conditions by attempting to bolster perceptions of his personal image by accenting his economic policies to convey decisive leadership while spotlighting diplomatic initiatives to project personal warmth.

Instead of presidents treating citizens as principals, they invest enormous resources in steering what the public focuses on. Their efforts to prime their image highlight a potentially fundamental barrier to citizens restraining elected officials—sophisticated efforts by politicians to track and then prime selected personality traits widen their discretion over policy and distance their decision making from the control of voters.

Citizen control is threatened by political strategies not only to prime Americans but also more fundamentally to manipulate their preferences when it comes to government policies. The intent to move public opinion is an enduring pattern throughout American history (Riker 1996; Jacobs and Shapiro 2000; Jacobs 2005, in press). The daunting question is whether the determined intent of political elites and presidents to move public opinion succeeds. Chapter 6 investigates a case (Lyndon Johnson) that favors presidential success—intense White House dedication and investment in molding public opinion along with a focus on policy areas about which the public lacks everyday information (foreign policy). Johnson did succeed in manipulating, but only in selected circumstances—he persuaded the public to support his Vietnam policy in its early stages before its enormous costs became apparent, but he was unable to change public policy attitudes permanently. In addition, he was able to prime the public to change the importance it attached to particular issues (especially poverty reduction and foreign affairs), but even these more modest effects were also selective and conditional.

Johnson's mixed record is consistent with the broader body of research on presidential public promotion (Rottinghaus 2012; Edwards 2003, 2007). The evidence of presidential impacts on opinion is clearest and most consistent—as in the Johnson case—with regard to influencing the public's ranking of what issues are most important. Jeffrey Cohen (1995) concludes from his investigation of State of the Union addresses that "merely mentioning a problem to the public heightens public concern with the policy problem" (102; see also Druckman and Holmes 2004). A president may decide to frequently mention reports of expanding employment in order to prompt Americans to focus on booming jobs rather than another issue as they evaluate him (Druckman 2004). In addition to studies of presidential influence, there is a broader body of research on the effects of candidates on what issues the public considers important (Berelson, Lazarsfeld, and McPhee 1954, 253–73; Jacobs and Shapiro 1994; Jacoby 1998; Johnston, Blais, Brady, and Crete 1992; Page 1978; Petrocik 1996; Riker 1996; Sellers 1998).

In contrast to findings of presidential (or candidate) influence on which issues are ranked as important, there is scant evidence that politicians are successful in persuading the public to change its policy preferences to support their positions. George Edwards concludes that the White House's enormous efforts to move the public's policy preferences generally fall on "deaf ears" (2003). The conclusion of recent reviews of presidential effects is that "presidents find difficulty in leading public opinion" (Tedin, Rottinghaus, and Rodgers 2011, 506) and that their "effectiveness [is] more problematic [than is often assumed]" (Cameron and Park 2011, 443) and may backfire by spotlighting opposition (Jacobs 2013).

In short, breaking into the black box of secretive presidential strategizing uncovers chronic *intent* to manipulate—routine efforts by presidents to change public opinion to support their priorities and policy positions. Although success is selective and conditional, evidence that presidents aim to shirk citizen control (rather than serve as mandated agents) shakes the foundations of classic democratic theories of representation.

## Reviving Representation

Evidence of the manipulative intent of elites to move public opinion and their selective success supports a growing body of critical democratic theory that challenges the responsiveness account and its analytic value as a standard for judging representative systems. The challenge is to incorporate both the constraints imposed by the unequal distribution of power and resources and the opportunities for accountability—wide access to diverse information and struggles for government power that can be competitive and consequential for collective decision making. Neopolyarchy in conjunction with new thinking about representation as a form of mobilization offers a fresh way to think about democratic governance—one that corrects the mistaken assumptions of politicians as passive responders while retaining appreciation for the spaces of meaningful citizen engagement with and democratic influence on governing elites.

## Democratic Theory Challenges to the Responsiveness Account

Nearly six decades ago, Anthony Downs (1957) placed competing candidates at the center of his model. In the context of postwar America with two parties fighting for voters who mostly congregated between the liberal and the conservative poles of the policy continuum, Downs's model predicted that candidates for elective office would pursue a strategy of locking down their base of support and then converging toward the policy preferences of median voters (see also Black 1958). Eulau, Wahlke, Buchanan, and Ferguson (1959) refined the expected effects of elections on candidates—and government officials anticipating their next campaign— along a continuum from the most responsive "mandated delegates" to the "independent trustees" who followed their judgment about advancing the national interest (rather than public opinion). The delegate/trustee framework motivated generations of studies regarding the degree of government responsiveness.[1] Mansbridge (2003, 518) encapsulates the one-way conceptual logic of this research: the "voter's power works forward" to hold representatives to the promises they made at election time.

Our evidence—along with that of a growing number of studies— challenges the anchors of the responsiveness model and opens the door to two fundamental challenges by critical democratic theorists to the prevailing conception of political representation.

FORECLOSING CITIZEN JUDGMENT. Lisa Disch (2011, 4–5) points to evidence that public preferences "fluctuate in response to politicians' and pollsters' choice of language," concluding that voter opinion "cannot serve as a *basis* for responsiveness." The implication, Disch argues, is that "political representation need not and cannot take preferences as its starting place" and that democratic theorists must instead "conceive of the 'people,' democracy's political subject, as endogenous to the process of representation."

Recasting theory on the premise that citizen preferences are always endogenous eviscerates the one-way sequencing· of the responsiveness account and opens the way for a series of withering critiques of the canonical theories of representation. To begin with, sorting politicians into delegate/trustee silos mistakenly assumes that public opinion is the primal force that mandates government decisions or that officials resist. Ignored is the financial, organizational, and political power that political elites and special interests devote to subverting representation by converting elected delegates into transmitters of manufactured opinion advancing favored interests and by capturing policymakers who deflect scrutiny by donning the cape of the trustee—the paragon of independent judgment about the national interest.

Disch undercuts Hannah Pitkin's (1967) previously revered analysis for "conceiv[ing of citizens] as capable of action and judgment." Evidence that individual judgment is "foreclosed" by elite framing and priming leads her to presume that "there is no trusting that citizens' objection or non-objection has not simply been framed or primed out of the debate by habit, ignorance, or stereotype" (Disch 2011, 8). Jane Mansbridge similarly pulls the legs out from under notions of representation that assumed citizen autonomy; she insists that political elites are "active . . . in searching out and sometimes creating [citizen preferences]" (Mansbridge 2003, 1; see also Young 2000; and Plotke 1997).

Treating citizen preferences as "necessarily endogenous to politics" also recasts debates about democratic deliberation and, specifically, Jürgen Habermas's effort to separate out "communicative action" as making possible reason-based public talk and opinion formation. Disch (2011, 2) disputes this concept of free-flowing and noncoercive communication for ignoring the normative implications of today's "information contexts where power is at stake and where unstated motives exist" (see also Jacobs and Shapiro 2000, 384–85, n. 5). In short, Disch (2011, 2013) pioneers a new generation of democratic theory that takes seriously the strategic realities of politics and its normative significance for citizenship.

ELITE STRATEGIES TO WIN BY MANIPULATING.   Critical democratic theorists pair their blow against classic models of representation for naively presuming that citizens act as autonomous sovereigns with a challenge to exalted conceptions of governors. Disch (2011, 2) insists that democratic theory must be reoriented to fully incorporate "strategic action by elites" who build their "bid for power . . . [on] recruit[ing] [public opinion] into

a winning majority." In other words, contemporary politicians jump the
one-way sequence—assumed by classic representation theory and the
responsiveness account—by placing their preferences first and then seeking to move the preferences of voters. Disch pushes back against both
Habermasian elevation of rationalistic communication and median voter
models that link motivation and responsiveness; she insists that " 'communicative' and 'strategic' action are linked inextricably." This shift not only
repositions citizens from independent actors to carriers of elite messages,
as suggested above; it also dethrones elected officials from their traditional perch as guardians protecting the national interest and faithfully
serving as median-vote responders to deceivers motivated to serve narrow
and particularistic ends.

## Contested Representation

How can the limitations of political representation spotlighted by critical democratic theory and new research be reconciled with concrete and
feasible opportunities for democratic life? Building a realistic model of
representation that is normatively guided and feasible in the real world of
American politics faces two hurdles. The first regards the quality or competence of citizens. How can the reality of routine elite attempts to move
public opinion during elections and policy disputes be integrated with the
agency of citizens and their enduring attitudes, beliefs, and understand-
ings of their interests? The second hurdle is controlling or diminishing the
threat of elites to monopolize public choices and dictate the formation of
quality citizen preference.

THE ENDURING CITIZEN.   Despite the intent of elites to manipulate and
their selective effects, generations of experience and research demonstrate durable, long-term public attitudes and beliefs regarding government policy, ideology, and other dimensions of citizen opinion (e.g.,
Stimson 1991; Page and Shapiro 1992). Newer research on "policy feed-
backs" demonstrates that ongoing experiences with specific government
programs such as Social Security contribute to the formation of public attitudes and the chronic updating and retrieving of them as individuals see
concrete benefits for themselves, family members, and others (Campbell
2003; Cook, Jacobs, and Kim 2010; Mettler and Soss 2004). Decades of
surveys show that nine of ten Americans support more or the same spending on Social Security with virtually no statistically significant variations

even in the face of harsh warnings of the program's impending bankruptcy and proposals for structural reform to save them (Cook and Jacobs 2002). For instance, George W. Bush boomeranged from his 2004 reelection into a year-long crusade to partially privatize Social Security that failed to dislodge these durable policy attitudes (Edwards 2007).

Political psychologists have drawn on social psychology to trace the changes that do occur in public opinion to the activation of long-held attitudes and beliefs rather than shifts in those basic views. Individuals rely on the mechanism of "online memory" to process large amounts of information in order to form immediate summary judgments ("running tallies") about policies, parties, and candidates that are then stored in long-term memory even as detailed considerations are lost (Lodge, McGraw, and Stroh 1989, 1990; Lodge and Stroh 1993). Through priming and framing, elites and the media can, under certain circumstances, trigger the selective retrieval from memory of stored policy attitudes, political attitudes, and judgments of candidates. The process of accessing stored attitudes and beliefs, however, does not guarantee elites success in moving citizens wherever they want: citizens often cling to stored opinions, especially in the face of contending communications from dueling political actors (Chong and Druckman 2007; Druckman, in press).

Critical democratic theorists astutely challenge classic notions of democratic representation that ignore elite efforts at manipulation (whether successful or not), but they confuse the selective and conditional retrieval of stored opinions with the utter absence of attitudes or beliefs. Disch (2011) suggests that public opinion is an epiphenomenon of elites, insisting that "there is no 'bedrock' . . . unadulterated preference" and that "citizens' capacity to form preferences depends on the self-interested communications of elites" and "the representative who seduced them into voicing a demand" (2, 10). Although individuals continually update their running tallies and are susceptible under certain circumstances to elite framing and priming, they do harbor enduring attitudes that are resistant to influence (and possible manipulation) and form the basis for reaching critical evaluations. Indeed, our research—and that of others—repeatedly reports the marginal effects of elites on public opinion, as revealed in our investigation of Lyndon Johnson and in findings that elite messages (including those from presidents) fall on "deaf ears" (Edwards 2003; Jacobs 2013).

The dilemma is to remain intensely watchful of elite distortions without losing sight of the empirical fact of meaningful, durable citizen attitudes and beliefs that can serve, under certain circumstances, as the basis for feasible forms of representation. The challenge is both to political theorists and to researchers who need to move from identifying the possibility of public opinion change to uncovering the precise conditions of opinion movement and the normative implications of those changes. Indeed, as mentioned, manipulation requires identifying the intent of politicians to move public opinion as well as analytically comparing changes in opinions to an agreed-on counterfactual that isolates "manipulated opinions"—a consensus on what that counterfactual should be has evaded theorists and empirical scholars for over a half century (Druckman, in press). We have clearly shown the intent of presidents and the conditions that enable their influence; when this reflects manipulation is a question of pressing relevance.

THE COUNTERVAILING EFFECTS OF ELITE COMPETITION.   Our focus on the threat of governing elites to American democracy echoes long-standing warnings of a coordinated power elite that monopolizes decision making across American society and the tendency of organized groups to cooperate with government officials to limit the government agenda to safe issues and cut insider deals (Mills 1956; Lowi 1969; Schattschneider 1960). The question, however, that has beguiled generations is how to control or, more realistically, mitigate the threat of elites, especially as they attempt to short-circuit democratic checks by manipulating citizens into supporting their narrow interests.

Critical democratic theory proposes a mobilization strategy to contest elite claims to embody the popular will (Disch 2011). Bryan Garsten (2009) ties the future of democracy to processes that "multiply and challenge governmental claims to represent the people" in order to "mak[e] any particular claim to fully represent the people implausible and . . . hel[p] combat the use of such claims to justify the concentration of power" (91). "Recruiting" broader and more inclusive voices of dissent would, according to Disch (2011), "mitigate passive absorption of elite communications" (12).

Mobilizing broad publics to contest elites by widening the "scope of conflict" (Schattschneider 1960) can be an effective strategy, but it lacks a strong record of effectiveness against routine, often-quiet processes that insinuate themselves into the scattered parts of government and dominate substantial parts of public decision making. Theodore Lowi (1969) and others traced the potency of organized interests who—in near

silence—allied with subunits in Congress and the bureaucracy to dominate silos of policy as varied as subsidies for sugar beets and defense con-
tracts (Ripley 1978). More recently, Hacker and Pierson (2010) report
that government policymaking is slanted toward corporate businesses and
affluent professional associations. Against the well-organized alliances of
elites motivated to reap intense, concentrated gains, the broad public is
disadvantaged in taking collective action on government policies that are,
in the abstract, important and substantial but deliver diffuse and nonsalient benefits to a dispersed public (Olson 1971).

Efforts to restrain elites require an auxiliary to periodic mobilization.
Elite competition is a feasible second mechanism for stemming control by
any one faction through two processes. One is the countervailing effects
of contending factions that minimize the potential of any one to dominate as a general rule. The offsetting effects of elite competition are most
commonly associated in the context of American politics with pluralism
(Truman 1951; Dahl 1956). Pluralism fails as an encompassing framework
because, among other reasons, not all interests are organized or compa-
rably represented (Schattschneider 1960; Strolovitch 2007). Nonetheless,
the countervailing dynamics of elite contestation stand out as a potentially
effective tool for checking elites—from impeding the inertial expansion
of bureaucracy (Weber 1978) to selecting among competing candidates
for office (Schumpeter 1950).

Elite competition is not only a negative process (the counteracting of
one faction by another) but also positive one—motivating elites to vie for
the support of citizens. The median voter theory has been criticized for
predicting responsiveness to majority opinion without due attention to
the theory's conditions—unimodal distribution of voters near the midpoint between the liberal and the conservative policy positions (Downs
1957). The reality of American politics differs significantly: national and
many statewide elections are defined by bipolar distributions of most voters near liberal and conservative positions, while many legislative races
occur in districts where most voters bunch near one ideological extreme
(Jacobs and Shapiro 2000; Wood 2009). Spatial voting theory predicts responsiveness to these distinct distributions of voters; it does not specify
a universal law of following majority opinion (especially in the context
of American election rules). The crucial insight, then, from spatial voting theory is that elite competition for voters increases the incentives to
locate and move toward the public's policy preferences (however they are
distributed).

The competition for voters—especially in circumstances where winning ideological supporters is not adequate to prevail—may induce receptiveness to enduring public opinion on salient issues. Our research and that of others shows that politicians seeking the support of voters outside their ideological core turn to well-crafted public presentations to attempt to move public opinion, but these efforts rarely proceed without rivals marshaling their own public case. The resulting counterframes often offset each other and fail to move voters (Druckman 2004). As elections approach and opinion-moving strategies prove ineffective, politicians face rising incentives to attend to sustained policy preferences of key voting blocs not locked down by either party.

Elite competition and the "mobilization" perspective of democratic theorists may interact. The fight for voters by rival political factions may generate incentives to activate otherwise submerged conflicts, boost citizens' awareness of their stakes, and lift participation. Where new constituencies are recruited, this may reconfigure the terms of elite competition. This dialectic has played out over the course of American political history: Reagan's recruitment of evangelicals sparked a two-decade battle for the "faith voter," while Barack Obama's election victories achieved by mobilizing younger voters, Hispanics, and people of color are intensifying competition between—and within—the Democratic and Republican Parties.

*Neopolyarchy*

Robert Dahl's concept of polyarchy offers a conceptual platform with which to identify the conditions for retaining and strengthening citizen engagement and reviving a form of representation that constrains decision makers in a large, dispersed society beset by elite attempts to manipulate citizens. In broad terms, Dahl (1984) defines *polyarchy* as a "system of political control" with multiple centers of power that enables "nonleaders [to] exercise a relatively high degree of control over leaders" (227, 230). Its utility is as a theory of democracy that supplies working tools to assess and promote achievable, though imperfect, conditions both for quality citizenship and for a form of elite governing that is constrained from obtaining dominance and motivated to vie for citizen support.

Polyarchy's attention to the potentially useful effects of elite competition needs to be bolstered with scrutiny of how senior government officials and their allies work—often within legal frameworks that formally guarantee political and civil rights—to mute, redirect, or altogether block citizen engagement and democratic representation. Our revitalized conception of democracy builds on but also moves beyond Dahl's polyarchy; we discuss three potential arenas for reinvigorating democracy.

DELIBERATION AND CITIZENSHIP. The first arena concerns the quality of citizenship that flows from the right to free expression and to access to diverse sources of information. Dahl equates polyarchy, in part, with a vibrant civil society in which citizens enjoy institutionally protected rights to assemble, exercise free speech, and obtain and develop information outside government sources. Working democracy requires public deliberation—whether face-to-face, through social media, or mediated through the press—about issues of community concern (including criticism of government). Even as public deliberation falls short of idealized standards of inclusivity and reason, it often contributes to the formation of citizen preferences and the communication of the stakes of policy choices.

How effectively public deliberation contributes to vibrant citizens who are alert to their stakes in political and policy debates has affected the transformation of communication. Individual citizens can now produce and search out information in ways that were previously precluded. Nonetheless, the new information age also replaced the common square with sources tied to partisan and ideological perspectives that reinforce and cater to the existing biases and attitudes of individuals (Prior 2007; Jacobs and Shapiro 2011; Druckman, Fein, and Leeper 2012; Lodge and Taber 2013). Formal rights and ample information independent of government control are key conditions for generating reasoned and inclusive deliberation through the media (Page 1996) and through face-to-face forums, personal interactions, and online communications (Jacobs, Cook, and Delli Carpini 2009). Whether citizens develop adequate understanding to assess the importance of the problems facing society, form reasoned assessments of their interests and preferences, and effectively participate politically are open questions that define the scope of working democracy and the agenda of reform.

Improving the quality of citizenship depends, as John Dewey observed, on the "improvement of the methods and conditions of debate, discussion, and persuasion" (2008, 365). Improvement as mass communication enters a transformed era will require inventive approaches to generating and contesting information as well as steps to accelerate the redesign of cities and localities to embed requirements that school boards, civil reviews of

police, and other agencies institutionalize meaningful public deliberation
into their decision making (Jacobs, Cook, and Delli Carpini 2009; Fung
2004). In addition, the new information age appears to be opening up possibilities for organized discursive mobilization to contest one-sided frames
(Druckman 2004; Disch 2012).

Treating the quality of citizenship as problematic acknowledges the
manipulative intent of elites while leaving open the definition of engaged
citizenship and the nature of meaningful education of the public under
certain conditions and in specific episodes (Druckman, in press; Jacobs,
Cook, and Delli Carpini 2009).

ELITE COMPETITION AND ACCOUNTABILITY.   The second arena for building
working democracy, according to polyarchy, concerns elite competition
and, specifically, the scrum of independent associations devoted to a variety of civic and political purposes. Dahl recognized—increasingly over
the course of his career—that the formal rights of individuals to form
relatively independent associations, interest groups, and political organizations were unequally exercised (Dahl 1985). Associations and interest
groups representing business and professional associations are better organized, funded, and positioned than consumers, public interest groups,
and advocates for the less well off to give voice to their interests (Schlozman and Tierney 1986; Verba, Schlozman, and Brady 1995; Berry 1999).

The associational advantage of the better off can, in certain circumstances, be mitigated by the formation and activism of "encompassing organizations" such as AARP (Olson 1982) or programmatically oriented
political parties (Schattschneider 1960; Jacobs 2014). For instance, President Bush's campaign to partially privatize Social Security originated in
proposals by financial interests and was promoted by them, but AARP
effectively countered, mobilizing seniors, and unnerving legislators to the
point that the president's party in Congress was unwilling even to bring his
proposal up for a vote in committee (Jacobs 2010).

New coalitions, inventive reorganizations, and new media foster opportunities to leverage resources (numbers and interconnections) and improve the presence and influence of underrepresented groups (see McCall
2013). The 2010 health reform, for instance, overcame efforts by insurers
to block it (as they have for decades) by mobilizing general practitioners
concerned with patients, hospitals weighed down by uncompensated care,
and organizations of patients and those lacking insurance (Jacobs and
Skocpol 2012; Kirsch 2012). Activists for environmental issues as well as

organized labor are similarly building advocacy coalitions and leveraging the tools of the new information age to confront one-sided frames.

MAKING ELECTIONS SCARY. The third arena of working democracy is electoral and, according to polyarchy, is defined by two dimensions: a high degree of public contestation (defined by free, frequent, and fair, competitive elections) and wide inclusiveness (namely, adults generally enjoy universal suffrage and the right to run for office) (Dahl 1971). Significant competition among politicians and candidates generates a process that Dahl expects to "hold [officeholders] more or less accountable through elections by dismissing them . . . in subsequent elections" (Dahl 2005, 193) or through their "expectations as to the reactions of the group of politically active citizens who go to the polls" (Dahl 1956, 72).

Not surprisingly, the actual practice in the United States falls short of ideal inclusive and accountable elections owing to the disenfranchisement of felons, the sway of party activists on nominations, partisan gerrymandering of legislative districts, the overrepresentation in the Senate of small states, and the comparatively exceptional administrative hurdles to registering and casting a ballot.[2] In addition, the most active voters tend to harbor single-issue commitments and ideological dispositions that may, in contemporary America's political party system, tend to pressure lawmakers to move away from centrist voters in a liberal and, especially, conservative direction.

Even with these significant limitations, however, centrist voters continue to swing presidential and certain state races, fueling competition and some accountability regarding issues not firmly staked out in party platforms. President Bush, for instance, prepared for his 2004 reelection campaign by pushing congressional conservatives to approve a substantial expansion of Medicare to cover prescription drug benefits in order to appeal to seniors and independents.

Electoral competition among dueling teams of elites may be intensifying efforts to mobilize new groups of citizens. For several decades after the 1970s, the political parties shifted resources from grassroots campaigning and toward capital-intensive advertising strategies. The twenty-first century has witnessed a renewed investment in grassroots organizing that leverages new technology to target individual voters with tailored information and to build webs of community ties, yielding a potentially potent combination of efficiency with the effectiveness of personal contact (Gerber and Green 2000). Many more steps can be taken, as they are being taken around the world, to institutionalize mechanisms that use elections to widen access for more diverse voices.

Our understanding and practice of representative democracy needs to change to keep up with the expanding institutional capacity of government and established interests to attempt to move public opinion and marginalize citizens. The everyday forms of representation too often resemble a kabuki theater in which elites attempt to orchestrate the audience's reaction and then claim to respond to it.

It is time to break from the passive form of representation that empowers elites and institutions to "speak for" citizens (Pitkin 1967) and assumes a beneficent "re-presentation" of existing public views. These cherished images of American governance bear little resemblance to the strategizing that goes on within the inner sanctums of American governing elites.

Institutionalized conflict and the mobilization of citizens can feed off of each other, spreading across today's arenas of politics—from informational networks and organized associations to centers of economic and government decision making. The mobilization of new constituents should replace the passive expectations of responsiveness; the fierce engagement in the struggle among elites is an antidote to the naive notion that civic deliberation can exert a meaningful impact apart from government.

For too long, political and economic elites organized politics to contain and channel the form and degree of political participation to secure their interests and autonomy. It is time for a new democracy that replaces passive re-presentation with a revitalized citizenry at the center of elite struggles for power, recasting the terrain and terms of competition among rival centers of power, and elevating the distribution of power and resources into matters of routine public debate and contestation.

# Acknowledgments

Our work on this book began, in earnest, in the fall of 1999 at the University of Minnesota's Department of Political Science. Through the subsequent fifteen years of work, our collaboration evolved into more than an intellectual endeavor, becoming a personal and supportive friendship. A wonderful by-product was the scholarly evolution that saw the two of us, with quite distinct backgrounds, come to a common view of what we hoped this book could be.

Throughout the process one of the great pleasures of working on a book for so long was that we had the time to discuss its themes with colleagues and students and to reflect and think through their questions, challenges, and offerings. Imagine the bounty of advice and reactions we received over the years.

We have benefited from the feedback of colleagues at the annual professional meetings at which we have presented sections of this book. We are particularly grateful to the "Navigating Public Opinion" conference that Fay Lomax Cook, Jeff Manza, and Ben Page organized at Northwestern University in 2000. Thanks are also due to Peter Enns and Chris Wlezien for their "Conference on Homogeneity and Heterogeneity in Public Opinion" at Cornell University in 2008. Lisa Disch's working group of political theorists and empirical researchers that met in 2010 at the University of Michigan provided an unusual impetus to think across disciplinary silos.

A veritable army of students toiled away on this project. They saw bits of their work make it into papers and articles; they would be justified in wondering what would become of the fuller project. This book is a testament to their hard work and trust that our many requests would bear fruit. Thanks to Patrick Carter, Adam Chelseth, Bas van Doorn, Thomas

Durfee, Brian Harrison, Melinda Jackson, Lauren Matecki, Thomas Leeper, Joshua Robison, Brandon Thompson, and Jonathan Weber. We are particularly grateful to Melanie Burns and Eric Ostermeier for their contributions.

Robert Eisinger supplied valuable feedback on an earlier version of this manuscript. We are especially grateful to our former colleague and ongoing interlocutor Lisa Disch, who has taught us a lot by skillfully walking the tightrope between empirical research on American politics and democratic theory.

Over the years, we have benefited from ongoing dialogues—in print and in person—with Jeff Cohen, George Edwards, Bob Erickson, John Geer, Jeff Manza, Ben Page, Jim Stimson, and Terry Sullivan. We are especially grateful to Bob Shapiro for his research on the core themes of this book—including an early version of the analysis that appears in chapter 6—and his extraordinary collegiality.

John Tryneski was an inspiration and taskmaster in bringing this project into book form. His keen intellect and high standards for fresh thinking have been a guiding light to the University of Chicago Press and the social science disciplines. We have both been extremely fortunate not only to benefit from his guidance on our work but also to work with him on various other projects. Our appreciation and recognition of our great luck in having John as a part of our own intellectual development is why we gratefully dedicate the book to him.

As much as we have gained from the contributions of colleagues and students, we also want to fully accept responsibility for this book's analyses and interpretations.

We now come to our families, who are due an apology for whatever distraction this project caused and a hearty thank-you for their patience. Indeed, our kids grew and developed at rates that exceeded our work on this book! We hope you find some measure of justification in this book.

# Notes

All microfilm citations are taken from the series *Political Activities of the Johnson White House* (Frederick, MD: University Publications of America, 1988). Please note also that the following abbreviations are used throughout the notes:

Johnson Library = Lyndon Baines Johnson Presidential Library, Austin, TX
Nixon Library = Nixon Presidential Library and Museum, Yorba Linda, CA
Reagan Library = Ronald Reagan Presidential Foundation and Library, Simi Valley, CA

## Introduction

1. Federalist Papers, no. 51, *New York Packet*, February 8, 1788, http://thomas.loc.gov/home/histdox/fed_51.html.

2. Federalist Papers, no. 10, *New York Packet*, November 23, 1787, http://thomas.loc.gov/home/histdox/fed_10.html.

3. Ibid.

4. Federalist Papers, no. 68, *New York Packet*, March 14, 1788, http://thomas.loc.gov/home/histdox/fed_68.html.

5. Federalist Papers, no. 70, *New York Packet*, March 14, 1788, http://thomas.loc.gov/home/histdox/fed_70-2.html.

6. Federalist Papers, no. 71, *New York Packet*, March 18, 1788, http://thomas.loc.gov/home/histdox/fed_71.html.

7. Edmund Burke, Speech to the Electors of Bristol, November 3, 1774, http://press-pubs.uchicago.edu/founders/documents/v1ch13s7.html.

8. Federalist Papers, no. 10.

9. "Federal Farmer," letter 7, December 31, 1787, http://www.constitution.org/afp/fedfar07.htm.

10. "Cato," letter 7, *New York Journal*, December 31, 1787, http://www.constitution.org/afp/cato_07.htm.

11. "Federal Farmer," letter 7.

12. William Jennings Bryan, "Cross of Gold" speech, July 9, 1896, http://history matters.gmu.edu/d/5354.

13. Theodore Roosevelt, "At the Laying of the Corner-Stone of the Pilgrim Memorial Monument, Provincetown, Massachusetts," August 20, 1907, http://www.theodore-roosevelt.com/images/research/txtspeeches/257.txt.

### Chapter One

1. While scholars debate whether candidates are most advantaged by matching citizens' exact issue position or by taking more extreme positions (see Merrill and Grofman 1999), the logic and motivation captured by the median voter theory continues to dominate.

2. Federalist Papers, no. 10.

3. We draw on previous research on presidential polling that we conducted together (Druckman and Jacobs 2006, 2011; Druckman, Jacobs, and Ostermeier 2004) and separately (Jacobs 1992a, 1992b, 1993; Jacobs and Shapiro 1994, 1995a, 1995b, 1999, 2000; Jacobs and Burns 2004). This book relies, however, on new data, updated or recoded variables, and reinterpretations; chapter 6 and sections of chapters 3–5 are entirely new.

### Chapter Two

1. Memo to LBJ from Panzer, March 25, 1968, Panzer, box 220, Memo to Redmon from Cantril re Harris Surveys, July 14, 1966, Panzer, box 395, and Memo to LBJ from Panzer, December 29, 1967, Watson, box 12, Johnson Library.

2. Memo from Nixon to Haldeman, December 30, 1969, HRH, box 403, Memo to Jeb MacGruder from Haldeman, January 21, 1970, HRH, box 403, Memo to Haldeman from Nixon, March 2, 1970, PPF, box 2, Memo to Haldeman from Larry Higby, April 7, 1970, HRH, box 403, Memo to Haldeman from Nixon, May 25, 1970, Bull, box 5C, and Interview with David Derge, May 17, 1993, Nixon Library.

3. Of particular influence was Berlo, Lemert, and Mertz (1969). See also Public Opinion Survey, "Illinois Statewide I," December 1971, p. 42, HRH, box 381, Nixon Library.

4. Note Attached to Memo to President from Watson re Fort Worth, TX, Survey by J. Richard Cookerly, July 17, 1967, Panzer, box 223; Interview with Fred Panzer by Lawrence R. Jacobs, November 12, 1992, in possession of the author; Memo to LBJ from Kinter, June 27, 1966, CFPR16, box 81, Johnson Library. Under the Kennedy administration, the only major official who seems to have come into regular contact with the polling data was Robert Kennedy. Under the Johnson

administration, six members of the White House staff were at various times involved in the polling operation: Bill Moyers and W. Marvin Watson, who were responsible for it, and the four junior staff members Fred Panzer, Hayes Redmon, Tad Cantril, and Richard Nelson.

5. The one-year period was from September 1965 to September 1966, when Johnson received more than seventy polls. Although most of his polling was done during his 1964 election campaign, the 1965–66 period was not unusual.

6. Memo from Strachan to Higby, Bruce Kehrli, and Secretarial Staff, re Checklist for "proper processing and control of poll information," June 14, 1971, HRH, box 334, Handwritten Notes between Higby and Tom Benham (Executive Vice President of ORC), April 13, 1971, HRH, box 334, Memo to File re April 13, 1971, Meeting of Behnam, Higby, and Strachan, May 19, 1971, HRH, box 334, Memo from Higby to John Brown, re Nixon's Insistence That Polls Be Included in Folders for His Trips, October 22, 1970, HRH, box 353, Memo from Higby to Strachan, May 5, 1971, HRH, box 353, Memo from Higby to Strachan, July 20, 1971, HRH box 335, Memo from Strachan to Haldeman, March 9, 1972, HRH 362, and Memo from Haldeman to Ehrlichman, September 12, 1972, HRH 363, Nixon Library.

7. Haldeman Diary, May 31, 1971 (Haldeman 1994).

8. Memo from Strachan to Haldeman, August 27, 1971, HRH, box 359, Nixon Library.

9. Under Nixon's instructions, the White House and, specifically, Haldeman closely supervised the polling by the Reelection Committee; Nixon also had Haldeman conduct polls that were independent of the Reelection Committee and secret. Memo to MacGruder from Teeter, November 17, 1971, HRH box 368, Memo from Higby to Haldeman re "Poll Plan," December 9, 1970, HRH, box 263, Memo (Draft), "Polling Memo" (drafted apparently by Haldeman's staff and eventually addressed to John Mitchell, who headed the reelection committee), n.d., HRH, box 263, Memo to John Mitchell from Jeb MaGruder and Larry Higby, June 8, 1971, HRH box 263, Memo to Mitchell and Haldeman from MaGruder and Higby, June 23, 1971, HRH, box 341, and Memo to Mitchell from Teeter, April 17, 1972, HRH box 362, Nixon Library.

10. Interview with Harry Dent by Lawrence R. Jacobs, May 26, 1993, in possession of the author.

11. The Nixon White House and its polling operation relied initially on the political scientist David Derge and, more significantly, on Fred Steeper, a survey methodologist trained at the University of Michigan's Institute for Social Research.

12. Memo to Mitchell from Flanigan, September 30, 1971, HRH, box 368, Nixon Library.

13. We use the White House private polling data to examine how presidents and their aides think about public opinion and design strategies. We do not consider the validity of White House private polling data in fully and accurately measuring public opinion, though the scope and quality of these data are striking and

2. Some issues evaded identification of ideological direction (e.g., it was unclear which direction indicated a conservative position). We exclude these issues from our analyses. Neutral statements constitute 8.4 percent of Nixon's public comments and 22.9 percent of Reagan's.

3. We do not impute missing values in any of our analyses. Our decision was based on an examination of archival and other evidence suggesting that presidents and their aides did not try to impute missing data and, thus, that any such imputed data cannot be expected to affect presidential behavior.

4. The interval between presidential statements and prior polling data was generally brief. (Details are available from the authors.) Also, we do not include policy dummy variables because our Policy Opinion data change over time very slowly or not at all. In this situation, it is preferable not to use policy dummies so as to ensure analysis of between-unit effects (see Beck 2001, 285).

5. There are inadequate data to test adequately the two remaining scenarios. We do not have data to test the independent scenario because Nixon and Reagan rarely made public statements without information on public opinion. Similarly, the pure disaggregation scenario is so rarely pursued that statistical analyses would not be informative (also see Druckman and Jacobs 2006).

6. The number of cases reported in table 3.2 below is slightly lower than that reported in table 3.1 above owing to missing lag values for the dependent variable.

7. Our results here for Nixon differ a bit from our previous findings because our current data set includes both foreign and domestic policy. Our past research on Nixon was limited to domestic policy only (see Druckman and Jacobs 2006).

8. More precisely, Reagan's average statement moved from 3.45 to 4.21. We computed these figures using Clarify (Tomz, Wittenberg, and King 2003), holding other variables at mean values (and, for each model, computing means based on the data analyzed in the given model). We rely on 5 percent shifts in each direction as the standard deviation for overall Ideological Identification is about 5 percent and past work has relied on one standard deviation changes (e.g., Soroka and Wlezien 2010, 97). (Details on the computations as well as standard errors—for this and other substantive interpretations throughout the book—are available from the authors.)

9. Druckman and Jacobs (2006, tables 4–6) provide more details about the general pattern of White House polling both reflecting and influencing its political strategy.

10. On issues for which Nixon collected Policy Opinion data, the average importance score, one month prior to data collection, was 7.23 percent (SD = 6.67 percent, $N = 245$), as compared to an average score of 2.21 percent (SD = 1.82 percent, $N = 242$) ($t_{485} = 11.30$, $p < .01$) on issues for which Nixon did not collect issue-specific data. The percentages are higher for Reagan in part because Nixon often asked for the most important issue besides Vietnam, whereas Reagan left it open.

11. For Reagan, the average importance score was lower (25 percent [SD = 23.20 percent, $N = 1,983$]) for issues about which he collected policy-specific data

than for those issues for which he did not (35.17 percent [SD = 25.90 percent, $N$ = 136]) ($t_{2117}$ = .42, $p$ < .70). This literally suggests that Reagan collected policy data on less important issues; a more sensible interpretation in conjunction with the full set of results is that importance was not a significant influence on Reagan.

12. On a five-point scale in which 5 is the most conservative, the average ideological direction of Nixon's statements was 2.55 (SD = 1.74, $N$ = 1,180), compared to 3.48 (SD = 1.80, $N$ = 2,516) for Reagan. This general pattern persisted across domestic and foreign policy domains.

13. When Reagan had data on specific policy issues, he made a statement 52 percent of the time; he made a statement only 19 percent of the time when he lacked issue-specific data. By comparison, Nixon was about equally prone to make a statement whether he had issue specific data (59 percent) or not (58 percent).

14. In Druckman and Jacobs (2006), we offer more detailed statistical analyses to show Nixon invested in Policy Opinion data on issues deemed publicly important while Reagan did so when he planned to address an issue.

15. Haldeman Diary, July 7, 1969 (Haldeman 1994); Memo to Mitchell from Teeter, March 3, 1972, HRH, box 362, "Position Paper: The 1972 Campaign," April 18, 1972, HRH, box 358, Memo to Chapin from Teeter (marked *Confidential*), July 25, 1972, HRH, box 363, and Memo to Mitchell from Teeter, May 11, 1972, HRH, box 362, Nixon Library. Additional analysis of ticket splitters was the central focal point of White House polling. Numerous archival records on it can be found in HRH, boxes 372, 380, 381, Nixon Library.

16. Haldeman Diary, May 7, 1969, April 2, 1970, January 17, 20, May 24, 28, June 2, 10, 27, July 17, August 1, 24, 31, 1971 (Haldeman 1994).

17. Haldeman Diary, July 11, 1970 (Haldeman 1994).

18. "The Public Appraises the Nixon Administration and Key Issues," Confidential Survey, ORC, December 1969, HRH, box 406, Nixon Library.

19. "Virginia Statewide Study (Volume I—Analysis)," February 1972, Market Opinion Research, HRH, box 380, Memo from Teeter to Mitchell, March 2, 1972, HRH, box 380, Memo from Higby to Strachan and Bruce Kehrli, September 6, 1971, HRH, box 335, and Memo, "Polls" (appears to be Higby's notes of a conversation with Haldeman following a conversation with the president), July 13, 1970, HRH, box 403, Nixon Library.

20. Memo to Derge from Higby, January 14, 1971, HRH, box 341; Memo from Nixon to Haldeman, December 30, 1969, HRH, box 403; Memo from Higby to Haldeman, December 9, 1970, HRH, box 262; and Memo to Mitchell from Teeter, April 17, 1972, HRH, box 362, Nixon Library.

21. Memo from Teeter to Haldeman, February 3, 1972, HRH, box 362, Nixon Library (emphasis added).

22. Memo to Mitchell from Teeter, "Final First Wave Analysis," May 11, 1972, HRH, box 362, Nixon Library.

23. Haldeman Diary, October 21, 1970, January 17, 1971 (Haldeman 1994); Memo to Haldeman from Teeter, August 8, 1972, HRH, box 363, Nixon Library.

24. Memo from Ehrlichman to Nixon, October 21, 1970, HRH, box 263, Nixon Library; Haldeman Diary, July 23, 1971 (Haldeman 1994).

25. Decision Making Information (DMI), "National Survey of Public Attitudes" (for the Republican National Committee), February 1981, Memo to Meese, Baker, and Deaver from Wirthlin re "The Social Security Issue," May 28, 1981, Memo to Meese, Baker, and Deaver from Wirthlin re "Present Perceptions of Ronald Reagan," May 28, 1981, DMI, "National Survey of Public Attitudes," for the Republican National Committee, May 1981, and Memo to Meese from Wirthlin re "Social Security," August 21, 1981, Chapman Files (DMI), box 5, Reagan Library.

**Chapter Four**

1. Federalist Papers, no. 71.

2. Federalist Papers, no. 10.

3. For a discussion of the president's pursuit of the nation's long-term interests as compared with Congress's parochial interests, see Tulis (1987, 39–40) and Moe (1985, 2003).

4. The proportion independent includes both "independent independents" as well as respondents who after declaring themselves as independent indicated that they were "closer" to one party.

5. Memo from Wirthlin to Rahrenkopf and Regan, February 7, 1985, Chapman Files (DMI), box 5, Memo from Wirthlin to Dick Richards, March 11, 1981, Elizabeth Dole Papers, box 6391, Memo from Ed Rollins to Don Regan, July 9, 1985, PR15, no. 317420, William Lacy to Regan, October 23, 1985, PR15, Wirthlin to Regan, February 12, 1986, PR15, and Roger Porter to Wirthlin, November 14, 1984, PR15, Reagan Library.

6. By contrast, Democratic leaders gravitated toward social and economic liberals who favored greater government intervention in market distributions, though the pressure to raise campaign contributions also placed a premium on higher-income groups among their supporters (Verba, Schlozman, and Brady 1995).

7. Memo to James Baker, Michael Deaver, Frank Fahrenkopf, Paul Laxalt, Ed Rollins, and Stuart Spencer from Wirthlin, July 26, 1984, Deaver Files, no. UA 115586; Wirthlin to Fahrenkopf and Regan, February 7, 1985, PR15; Memo from Wirthlin to Richard Allen re Mideast, August 21, 1981, PR15, no. 043822, Reagan Library.

8. "Gun Control Issue Forecast," September 21, 1981, Elizabeth Dole Files, OA 5455, Reagan Library.

9. Memo from Richard Beal to Edwin Meese, James Baker, Michael Deaver, and William Clark, March 12, 1982, Deaver Files, Reagan Library.

10. Memo to Meese, Baker, and Deaver from Wirthlin re "Reagan Performance," February 2, 1982, and Memo from Richard Beal to Edwin Meese, James

Baker, Michael Deaver, and William Clark, March 12, 1982, Deaver Files, Reagan Library.

11. Memo to Baker, Deaver, Fahrenkopf, Laxalt, Rollins, and Spencer from Wirthlin, July 26, 1984, Deaver Files, no. UA 115586, Reagan Library.

12. Untitled Memo, n.d., PR 15, document no. 213994, and Decision/Making/Information, "National Benchmark Survey of Public Attitudes" (for the Republican National Committee), November 1983, Chapman Files, box 29, Reagan Library.

13. Memo from Gary Bauer to Edwin Harper re "Polls on the Social Issues," March 29, 1982, PR15 (#093915), Reagan Library.

14. Memo to Baker, Deaver, Fahrenkopf, Laxalt, Rollins, and Spencer from Wirthlin, July 26, 1984, Deaver Files, no. UA 115586, Reagan Library.

15. Although the White House's measurement of these subgroup categories is neither consistent nor necessarily comparable with contemporary social science research standards, administration officials clearly treated information about these subgroups as valid and politically important (Druckman and Jacobs 2006).

16. Reagan measured income in two ways. Sometimes he asked respondents to classify themselves as low, middle, or upper class. Other times, he asked them to report which of three different earning categories they fall in (e.g., under $15,000 a year). We combined these measures by splitting the three numeric responses into three income-level groups—one below $15,000, one between $15,000 and $30,000, and one above $30,000. This seemed like the most sensible way to reconcile the two measures since each question form offered three response categories, so we ordered and combined them from low to high. In many cases, however, Reagan reported only data provided by the highest strata: of the data he collected, he segmented it nearly 60 percent of the time for high-income earners and only 32 percent for low-income people.

17. We align the data in table 4.1 with our later analysis of the impact of White House polling on Reagan's behavior. This means that the data are confined to cases where Reagan made a statement and possessed the relevant data as analyzed below (e.g., possessed Ideological Identification data). The number of separate poll results for the subgroups discussed here may differ from the number of observations in later regression analyses; the addition of variables may reduce the number of cases.

18. In particular, we regress Reagan's Policy Positions against lagged (one month) Policy Positions, lagged Ideological Identification (the percentage of conservatives, measured at least one month prior to the statement), and lagged Policy Opinion.

19. Our subgroup measures do not face the scale issues identified by Bhatti and Erikson (2011) since we do not multiply our measures by the percentage of respondents in each subgroup.

20. As in chapter 3, we computed these figures using Clarify, holding other variables at mean values (and for each model computing means on the basis of the

19. "Position Paper: The 1972 Campaign," April 18, 1972, HRH, box 358, and Memo to JNM from RMT re "Interim Analysis Report," April 17, 1972, HRH, box 362, Nixon Library.

20. We do not find analogous bifurcation in analyses with Nixon.


**Chapter Six**

1. This chapter examines a critical part of the process—the intent of an authoritative government official equipped with unrivaled institutional and public resources. A full understanding of manipulation requires a careful examination of both the intent of politicians and the preferences of citizens (see Druckman, in press).

2. Federalist Papers, no. 10.

3. Federalist Papers, no. 1, *Independent Journal*, October 27, 1787, http://thomas.loc.gov/home/histdox/fed_01.html.

4. Meet the Press, December 30, 2012, http://www.nbcnews.com/id/50314590/ns/meet_the_press-transcripts/#.URvRuCJkg_E.

5. Confidential Memo to M. W. Watson from N. Katzenbach, October 27, 1967, microfilm, Johnson Library.

6. Memo to Cater from E. Duggan, May 31, 1966, Ex PR18, box 358, Memo to Bill Moyers from Tom Johnson, August 10, 1966, Ex PR18, box 358, and Memo from Cater to LBJ, December 26, 1964, Ex PR18, box 356, Johnson Library.

7. Memo to Cater from E. Duggan, May 31, 1966, Ex PR18, box 358, Johnson Library.

8. Memo to LBJ from Moyers, June 9, 1966, LBJ, Moyers, box 12, Johnson Library.

9. White House efforts to use the executive branch to promote its accomplishments are contained in the following: Memo to LBJ from McPherson, December 1, 1965, McPherson, box 11, Memo to LBJ from W. M. Watson, May 31, 1967, Ex PR, box 1, Memo to LBJ from F. Panzer, January 21, 1967, Ex FG1, box 13, Memo to LBJ from D. Cater, March 28, 1968, Ex FG1, box 18, Memo to J. Jones from F. Kelly, December 30, 1966, Ex PR18, box 359, Memo from Redmon to Moyers, June 9, 1966, Moyers, box 12, Letter from LBJ to John Macy, n.d., Ex FG100/M, box 130, Memo to All Personnel Handling Correspondence, March 26, 1965, EX FG1, box 11, and Memo from Busby to Johnson, February 20, 1965, Ex FG100, box 130, Johnson Library.

10. White House aides were sufficiently taken by Lipset's analysis of presidential leadership when it came to public opinion on foreign policy matters that they forwarded it to the President. Memo to Moyers from Redmon, August 24, 1966, Moyers, box 12, and Memo to LBJ from Moyers, September 10, 1966, Ex PR16, Johnson Library. Altschuler (1990) offers a similar interpretation of White House leadership based on archival records.

11. Abe Fortas, November 5, 1967, quoted in Berman (1989, 106).

12. Memo to LBJ from Panzer, November 15, 1967, microfilm, reel 4, no. 965, Johnson Library.

13. Memo to LBJ from J. Gardner, December 19, 1966, Ex FG165, box 12, Memo from H. Redmon to B. Moyers, December 17, 1965, Panzer, box 217, Memo to Bundy, Moyers, Valenti, and Cater, December 14, 1965 (author not indicated), microfilm, reel 46, no. 124, and "A Survey of Political Climate in New York City," March 1965, by Oliver Quayle, Panzer File, box 186, Johnson Library.

14. Interview with Fred Panzer by Lawrence R. Jacobs, November 12, 1992, in possession of the author; Memo to Moyers from Redmon, August 24, 1966, Moyers, box 12, Johnson Library.

15. Memo to LBJ from Panzer, November 15, 1967, microfilm, reel 4, no. 965, Johnson Library.

16. Memo to LBJ from J. Gardner, December 19, 1966, Ex FG165, box 12, Memo from H. Redmon to B. Moyers, December 17, 1965, Panzer, box 217, Memo to Bundy, Moyers, Valenti, and Cater, December 14, 1965 (author not indicated), microfilm, reel 46, no. 124, and "A Survey of Political Climate in New York City," March 1965, by Oliver Quayle, Panzer File, box 186, Johnson Library.

17. See chapter 2, n. 24, above.

18. Memo to LBJ from J. Gardner, December 19, 1966, Ex FG165, box 12, Memo from H. Redmon to B. Moyers, December 17, 1965, Panzer, box 217, Memo to Bundy, Moyers, Valenti, and Cater (author not indicated), December 14, 1965, microfilm, reel 46, no. 124, and 186, "A Survey of Political Climate in New York City," March 1965, by Oliver Quayle, Panzer File, box 186, Johnson Library.

19. See chapter 2, n. 24, above.

20. Indeed, while we weighted by mentions in earlier chapters, we weight Johnson's policy positions by lines to capture the core theoretical concept of persuasion—the extensiveness of elite attention to moving the public's policy positions. This might include an issue that is not frequently mentioned but received extensive discussion when it was raised, as may happen in nationally televised presidential addresses.

21. By including the lagged dependent variable to control for potential unmeasured outside influences, our results are weaker; excluding it produces stronger effects.

22. We recognize that we are not controlling for such factors as media. In terms of media, however, there is nothing inconsistent in our model if it is the media mediating the relationship between Johnson's rhetoric and public opinion. We also recognize our failure to control for real-world events. The challenge here is that our coverage of the universe of topics on which Johnson spoke makes it unclear how we could go about identifying which events would matter on a particular issue. Finally, note that all the results we report below are robust to including issue-specific controls as well as time controls.

23. Using Clarify, we found that, if Johnson chose not to make any statement

on poverty in a given month and the prior month's opinion on the poverty issue was set at its mean level, the predicted public support for poverty programs is 50.19 (SE = 2.04). By contrast, if his weighted position on poverty reached his average (21.54), then support increased from 50.19 to 54.16 (SE = 1.56). This is a statistically significant change.

24. The $p$-value is .60.

25. Fine-tuned analyses did find priming effects during the isolated period when Johnson was popular early in his term and able to exert a priming effect on domestic policies other than poverty and Vietnam. These findings, however, appear to reflect the particular circumstances after Kennedy's assassination and the landslide 1964 contest—events that faded along with Johnson's approval and ability to prime.

26. See n. 23 above.

27. Memo to LBJ from Panzer, November 20, 1967, Panzer, box 223, Memo to LBJ from Panzer, November 14, 1967, Watson, box 15, and "A Study of Attitudes of Voters in Pennsylvania," by John Kraft Inc., November 1967, Watson, box 15, Johnson Library.

28. Memo to LBJ from B. Moyers, December 27, 1965, forwarding Memo to Moyers from H. Redmon, December 27, 1965, Moyers, box 11, Johnson Library.

29. Memo to Moyers from H. Redmon, February 23, 1966, Panzer, box 217, and Memo to Moyers from Redmon, September 27, 1966, Moyers, box 12, Johnson Library.

30. Telex to LBJ from Panzer, December 28, 1967, microfilm, Reel 41, Ex PR16, and Memo to LBJ from Panzer re National Quayle Survey, November 28, 1967, microfilm, Reel 41, Ex PR16, Johnson Library.

31. Memo to LBJ from Fred Panzer, march 8, 1968, microfilm, reel 41, Johnson Library.

**Chapter Seven**

1. Research on responsiveness includes these important studies: Miller and Stokes (1963); Page and Shapiro (1983); Bartels (1991); Achen (1977, 1978); Erikson (1978); Hill and Hurley (1999); Erikson, MacKuen, and Stimson (2002); and Erikson, Wright, and McIver (1989, 1993).

2. About one-fourth of the people in the United States are represented by sixty-two senators from less populated states, while another fourth are served by six senators from the largest states. See http://www.nytimes.com/interactive/2013/03/11/us/politics/small-state-advantage.html?_r=0.

# References

Achen, Christopher H. 1977. "Measuring Representation: Perils of the Correlation Coefficient." *American Journal of Political Science* 21:805–15.

———. 1978. "Measuring Representation." *American Journal of Political Science* 22:475–510.

Aldrich, John H. 1995. *Why Parties? The Origin and Transformation of Political Parties in America.* Chicago: University of Chicago Press.

Aldrich, John, and David Rhode. 1998. "Measuring Conditional Party Government." Typescript, Duke University, Political Science Department.

Aldrich, John H., John L. Sullivan, and Eugene Borgida. 1989. "Foreign Affairs and Issue Voting: Do Presidential Candidates 'Waltz Before a Blind Audience?'" *American Political Science Review* 83, no. 1:123–41.

Altschuler, Bruce E. 1990. *LBJ and the Polls.* Gainesville: University Press of Florida.

American Political Science Association Task Force. 2004. "American Democracy in an Age of Rising Inequality: Report of the American Political Science Association Task Force on Inequality and American Democracy." *Perspectives on Politics* 2, no. 4:651–66.

Andrews, Edmund. 2008. "Greenspan Concedes Error on Regulation." *New York Times*, October 23.

Ansolabehere, Stephen, Jonathan Rodden, and James M Snyder. 2008. "The Strength of Issues: Using Multiple Measures to Gauge Preference Stability, Ideological Constraint, and Issue Voting." *American Political Science Review* 102, no. 2:215–32.

Bachrach, Peter, and Morton Baratz. 1962. "Two Faces of Power." *American Political Science Review* 56, no. 4 (December): 947–52.

Barofsky, Neil. 2012. *Bailout: An Inside Account of How Washington Abandoned Main Street While Rescuing Wall Street.* New York: Free Press.

Bartels, Larry M. 1991. "Constituency Opinion and Congressional Policy Making: The Reagan Defense Buildup." *American Political Science Review* 85:457–74.

Cappella, Joseph N., and Kathleen H. Jamieson. 1997. *Spiral of Cynicism: The Press and the Public Good*. New York: Oxford University Press.

Carmines, Edward, and James Stimson. 1989. *Issue Evolution: Race and the Transformation of American Politics*. Princeton, NJ: Princeton University Press.

Carpenter, Daniel. 2011. "The Contest of Lobbies and Disciplines: Finance Politics and Regulatory Reform in the Obama Administration." In *Reaching for a New Deal: Ambitious Governance, Economic Meltdown, and Polarized Politics in Obama's First Two Years*, ed. Theda Skocpol and Lawrence Jacobs, 139–88. New York: Sage.

Carter, Shan, and Amanda Cox. 2011. "One 9/11 Tally: $3.3 Trillion." *New York Times*, September 8.

Chafe, William. 1986/2003. *The Unfinished Journey: America since World War II*. 5th ed. New York: Oxford University Press.

Chong, Dennis. 1996. "Creating Common Frames of Reference on Political Issues." In *Political Persuasion and Attitude Change*, ed. Diana C. Mutz, Paul M. Sniderman, and Richard A. Brody, 195–224. Ann Arbor: University of Michigan Press.

Chong, Dennis, and James N. Druckman. 2007. "Framing Public Opinion in Competitive Democracies." *American Political Science Review* 101, no. 4:637–55.

———. 2010. "Dynamic Public Opinion: Communication Effects over Time." *American Political Science Review* 104, 4:663–80.

———. 2011. "Public-Elite Interactions: Puzzles in Search of Researchers." In *The Oxford Handbook of the American Public Opinion and the Media*, ed. Robert Y. Shapiro, Lawrence R. Jacobs, and George C. Edwards III, 170–88. Oxford: Oxford University Press.

———. 2012. "Dynamics in Mass Communication Effects Research." In *The Sage Handbook of Political Communication*, ed. Holli Semetko and Maggie Scammell, 307–23. Los Angeles: Sage.

Claibourn, Michele P. 2008. "Making a Connection: Repetition and Priming in Presidential Campaigns." *Journal of Politics* 70, no. 4:1142–59.

Cohen, Jeffrey. 1995. "Presidential Rhetoric and the Public Agenda." *American Journal of Political Science* 39 (February): 87–107.

Converse, Philip. 1964. "The Nature of Belief Systems in Mass Publics." In *Ideology and Discontent*, ed. David Apter, 206–61. Glencoe, IL: Free Press.

Cook, Fay Lomax, and Lawrence R. Jacobs. 2002. "Assessing Assumptions about Attitudes toward Social Security: Popular Claims Meet Hard Data." In *The Future of Social Insurance: Incremental Action or Fundamental Reform*, ed. Peter Edelman, Dallas Salisbury, and Pamela Larson, 82–118. Washington, DC: Brookings Institution.

Cook, Fay Lomax, Lawrence Jacobs, and Dukhong Kim. 2010. "Trusting What You Know: Information, Knowledge, and Confidence in Social Security." *Journal of Politics* 72 (April): 1–16.

Cook, Fay L., Tom R. Tyler, Edward G. Goetz, Margaret T. Gordon, David L. Protess, Donna R. Leff, and Harvey L. Molotch. 1983. "Media and Agenda-Setting: Effects on the Public, Interest Group Leaders, Policy Makers, and Policy." *Public Opinion Quarterly* 47 (Spring): 16–35.

Cook, Thomas, and Donald Campbell. 1979. *Quasi-Experimentation: Design and Analysis Issues for Field Settings*. Boston: Houghton Mifflin.

Dahl, Robert. 1956. *A Preface to Democratic Theory*. Chicago: University of Chicago Press.

———. 1961. *Who Governs? Democracy and Power in an American City*. New Haven, CT: Yale University Press.

———. 1971. *Polyarchy: Participation and Opposition*. New Haven, CT: Yale University Press.

———. 1984. "Polyarchy, Pluralism, and Scale." *Scandinavian Political Studies*, n.s., 7, no 4 (December): 225–40. https://tidsskrift.dk/index.php/scandinavian_political_studies/article/view/12886/24569.

———. 1985. *A Preface to Economic Democracy*. Berkeley and Los Angeles: University of California Press.

———. 1989. *Democracy and Its Critics*. New Haven, CT: Yale University Press.

———. 2005. "What Political Institutions Does Large-Scale Democracy Require?" *Political Science Quarterly* 120 (Summer): 187–97.

Delli Carpini, Michael X., and Scott Keeter. 1996. *What Americans Know about Politics and Why It Matters*. New Haven, CT: Yale University Press.

DeRouen, Karl, Jr. 2000. "Presidents and the Diversionary Use of Force." *International Studies Quarterly* 44, no. 2 (June): 317–28.

Dewey, John. 2008. "The Public and Its Problems." In *John Dewey: The Later Works*, vol. 2, *1925–1927*, ed. Jo Ann Boydston and Bridget A. Walsh, 235–372. Carbondale: Southern Illinois University Press.

Disch, Lisa. 2011. "Toward a Mobilization Conception of Democratic Representation." *American Political Science Review* 105 (February): 100–114.

———. 2012. "Democratic Representation and the Constituency Paradox." *Perspectives on Politics* 10, no. 3:599–616.

———. 2013. "On the Benefits of 'Strategic Speech' for Deliberative Democracy." Paper presented at the workshop "Strategic Uses of Language: Politicizing Deliberative Democracy," University of British Columbia, June 14–15.

Downs, Anthony. 1957. *An Economic Theory of Democracy*. New York: Harper.

Druckman, James N. 2001. "The Implications of Framing Effects for Citizen Competence." *Political Behavior* 23, no. 3:225–56.

———. 2003. "The Power of Television Images: The First Kennedy-Nixon Debate Revisited." *Journal of Politics* 65, no. 2:559–71.

———. 2004. "Political Preference Formation: Competition, Deliberation, and the (Ir)relevance of Framing Effects." *American Political Science Review* 98, no. 4:671–86.

———. 2011. "Democratic Preferences: Criteria for Evaluating Citizen Competence." Typescript, Northwestern University, Department of Political Science.

———. In press. "Pathologies of Studying Public Opinion, Political Communication, and Democratic Responsiveness." *Political Communication.*

Druckman, James N., Jordan Fein, and Thomas J. Leeper. 2012. "A Source of Bias
in Public Opinion Stability." *American Political Science Review* 106:430–54.

Druckman, James N., and Justin W. Holmes. 2004. "Does Presidential Rhetoric
Matter? Priming and Presidential Approval." *Presidential Studies Quarterly*
34:755–78.

Druckman, James, and Lawrence Jacobs. 2006. "Lumpers and Splitters: The Public Opinion Information That Politicians Collect and Use." *Public Opinion
Quarterly* 70 (December): 453–76.

———. 2009. "Presidential Responsiveness to Public Opinion." In *The Oxford
Handbook of the American Presidency*, ed. George C. Edwards III and William G. Howell, 160–81. Oxford: Oxford University Press.

———. 2011. "Segmented Representation: The Reagan White House and Disproportionate Responsiveness." In *Who Gets Represented?* ed. Christopher
Wlezien and Peter Enns, 166–88. New York: Sage.

Druckman, James N., Lawrence R. Jacobs, and Eric Ostermeier. 2004. "Candidate Strategies to Prime Issues and Image." *Journal of Politics* 66 (November):
1205–27.

Druckman, James N., James H. Kuklinski, and Lee Sigelman. 2009. "The Unmet
Potential of Interdisciplinary Research: Political Psychological Approaches to
Voting and Public Opinion." *Political Behavior* 31, no. 4:485–510.

Druckman, James N., and Arthur Lupia. 2000. "Preference Formation." *Annual
Review of Political Science* 3:1–24.

———. 2006. "Mind, Will, and Choice: Lessons from Experiments in Contextual
Variation." In *The Oxford Handbook of Contextual Political Analysis*, ed. Robert E. Goodin and Charles Tilly, 97–113. Oxford: Oxford University Press.

Edelman, Murray. 1985. *The Symbolic Uses of Politics.* Chicago: University of Illinois Press.

Edsall, Mary, and Thomas Byrne Edsall. 1991. *Chain Reaction: The Impact of
Race, Rights, and Taxes on American Politics.* New York: Norton.

Edwards, George C., III. 1983. *The Public Presidency.* New York: Palgrave Mac-
millan.

———. 1989. *At the Margins: Presidential Leadership of Congress.* New Haven,
CT: Yale University Press.

———. 1996a. "The Presidential Pulpit: Bully or Baloney?" In *Understanding
the Presidency*, ed. James P. Pfiffner and Roger Davidson, 326–36. New York:
Harper Collins.

———. 1996b. "Presidential Rhetoric: What Difference Does It Make?" In *The
Future of the Rhetorical President*, ed. Martin J. Medhurst, 199–217. College
Station: Texas A&M University Press.

———. 2003. *On Deaf Ears: The Limits of the Bully Pulpit*. New Haven, CT: Yale University Press.

———. 2007. *Governing by Campaigning*. New York: Longman.

———. 2009. *The Strategic President: Persuasion and Opportunity in Presidential Leadership*. Princeton, NJ: Princeton University Press.

Eisinger, Robert. 2003. *The Evolution of Presidential Polling*. New York: Cambridge University Press.

Enelow, James, and Melvin Hinich. 1984. *The Spatial Theory of Voting*. Cambridge, MA: Cambridge University Press.

Enns, Peter K., and Christopher Wlezien. 2011. "Group Opinion and the Study of Representation." In *Who Gets Represented?* ed. Peter K. Enns and Christopher Wlezien, 1–26. New York: Sage.

Erikson, Robert S. 1978. "Constituency Opinion and Congressional Behavior: A Reexamination of the Miller-Stokes Data." *American Journal of Political Science* 22:511–35.

Erikson, Robert S., Michael B. MacKuen, and James A. Stimson. 2002. *The Macro Polity*. New York: Cambridge University Press.

Erikson, Robert, and David Romero. 1990. "Candidate Equilibrium and the Behavioral Model of the Vote." *American Political Science Review* 84:1103–26.

Erikson, Robert S., Gerald C. Wright Jr., and John P. McIver. 1989. "Political Parties, Public Opinion, and State Policy in the United States." *American Political Science Review* 83:728–50.

———. 1993. *Statehouse Democracy: Public Opinion and Policy in the American States*. Cambridge: Cambridge University Press.

Eulau, Heinz, John Wahlke, William Buchanan, and Leroy C. Ferguson. 1959. "The Role of the Representative: Some Empirical Observations on the Theory of Edmund Burke." *American Political Science Review* 53 (September): 742–56.

Fearon, James. 1999. "Electoral Accountability and the Control of Politicians." In *Democracy, Accountability, and Representation*, ed. Adam Przeworski, Bernard Manin, and Susan Stokes, 55–97. New York: Cambridge University Press.

Fenno, Richard. 1978. *Home Style: House Members in Their Districts*. Boston: Little, Brown.

Fernandes, Juliana. 2013. "Effects of Negative Political Advertising and Message Repetition on Candidate Evaluation." *Mass Communication and Society* 16, no. 2:268–91.

Fiorina, Morris. 1977. *Congress: Keystone of the Washington Establishment*. New Haven, CT: Yale University Press.

———. 1981. *Retrospective Voting in American National Elections*. New Haven, CT: Yale University Press.

Fisher, Louis. 1995/2004. *Presidential War Power*. 2nd ed. Lawrence: University Press of Kansas.

Fiske, Susan T. 1980. "Attention and Weight in Person Perception." *Journal of Personality and Social Psychology* 38:889–906.

Holsti, Ole. 2006. *Public Opinion and American Foreign Policy*. Ann Arbor: University of Michigan Press.

Horkheimer, Max, and Theodor Adorno. 1972. *Dialectic of Enlightenment*. New York: Continuum.

Huckfeldt, Robert, Peter Johnson, and John Sprague. 2004. *Political Disagreement: The Survival of Diverse Opinions within Communication Networks*. New York: Cambridge University Press.

Iraq and Afghanistan Casualty Count. n.d. http://icasualties.org.

Iyengar, Shanto. 1990. "Shortcuts to Political Knowledge: The Role of Selective Attention and Accessibility." In *Information and Democratic Processes*, ed. John A. Ferejohn and James H. Kuklinski, 160–85. Urbana: University of Illinois Press.

———. 2010. "Framing Research: The Next Steps." In *Winning with Words: The Origins and Impact of Political Framing*, ed. Brian F. Schaffner and Patrick J. Sellers, 185–91. New York: Routledge.

Iyengar, Shanto, and Donald R. Kinder. 1986. "More Than Meets the Eye: Tv News, Priming, and Public Evaluations of the President." In *Public Communication and Behavior* (2 vols.), ed. George Comstock, 1:136–74. New York: Academic.

———. 1987. *News That Matters*. Chicago: University of Chicago Press.

Jacobs, Lawrence. 1992a. "Institutions and Culture: Health Policy and Public Opinion in the U.S. and Britain." *World Politics* 44 (January): 179–209.

———. 1992b. "The Recoil Effect: Public Opinion and Policymaking in the U.S. and Britain." *Comparative Politics* 24 (January): 199–217.

———. 1993. *The Health of Nations: Public Opinion and the Making of Health Policy in the U.S. and Britain*. Ithaca, NY: Cornell University Press.

———. 2005. "Communicating from the White House: From Mass Communications to Specialized Constituencies." In *Presidents and Bureaucrats: The Executive Branch and American Democracy*, ed. Joel Aberbach and Mark Peterson, 174–217. Oxford: Oxford University Press.

———. 2009. "Building Reliable Theories of the Presidency." *Presidential Studies Quarterly* 39 (December): 771–80.

———. 2010. "The Presidency and the Press: The Paradox of the White House 'Communications War.'" In *The Presidency and the Political System* (9th ed.), ed. Michael Nelson, 323–57. Washington, DC: Congressional Quarterly Press.

———. 2011. "The Betrayal of Democracy: The Purpose of Public Opinion Survey Research and Its Misuse by Presidents." In *Manipulating Democracy*, ed. Wayne LeCheminant and John Parrish, 190–208. New York: Routledge.

———. 2013. "The Public Presidency and Disciplinary Presumptions." *Presidential Studies Quarterly* 43, no. 1:16–34.

———. 2014. "Political Parties and Economic Inequality." In *Political Parties*, ed. Marjorie Hershey, 396–407. Washington, DC: Congressional Quarterly Press.

————. In press. "Going Institutional: The Making of Political Communications." In *The Oxford Handbook of Political Communication*, ed. Kathleen Hall Jamieson and Kate Kenski. New York: Oxford University Press.

Jacobs, Lawrence, and Melanie Burns. 2004. "The Second Face of the Public Presidency: Presidential Polling and the Shift from Policy to Personality Polling." *Presidential Studies Quarterly* 34, no. 3 (Fall): 536–56.

Jacobs, Lawrence, Fay Lomax Cook, and Michael Delli Carpini. 2009. *Talking Together: Public Deliberation in America and the Search for Community*. Chicago: University of Chicago Press.

Jacobs, Lawrence, and Melinda Jackson. 2004. "Presidential Leadership and the Threat to Popular Sovereignty: Building an Appealing Image to Dodge Unpopular Policy Issues in the Nixon White House." In *Polls, Politics, and the Dilemmas of Democracy*, ed. Michael Genevese and Matt Streb, 29–54. Albany: State University of New York Press.

Jacobs, Lawrence, and Desmond King. 2012. "Concealed Advantage: The Federal Reserve's Financial Interventions After 2007." Paper prepared for the conference "Governing the Fed," Nuffield College, Oxford, October 5–6.

Jacobs, Lawrence, and Benjamin Page. 2005. "Who Influences U.S. Foreign Policy?" *American Political Science Review* 99 (February): 107–24.

Jacobs, Lawrence, Benjamin I. Page, Melanie Burns, Gregory McAvoy, and Eric Ostermeier. 2004. "What Presidents Talk About: The Nixon Case." *Presidential Studies Quarterly* 33, no. 4:751–71.

Jacobs, Lawrence R., and Robert Y. Shapiro. 1994. "Issues, Candidate Image and Priming: The Use of Private Polls in Kennedy's 1960 Presidential Campaign." *American Political Science Review* 88 (September): 527–40.

————. 1995a. "Presidential Manipulation of Public Opinion: The Nixon Administration and the Public Pollsters." *Political Science Quarterly* 10 (Winter): 519–38.

————. 1995b. "The Rise of Presidential Polling." *Public Opinion Quarterly* 59, no. 2 (Summer): 163–95.

————. 1999. "Lyndon Johnson, Vietnam, and Public Opinion: Rethinking Realists' Theory of Leadership." *Presidential Studies Quarterly* 29 (September): 592–616.

————. 2000. *Politicians Don't Pander: Political Manipulation and the Loss of Democratic Responsiveness*. Chicago: University of Chicago Press.

————. 2011. "Public Opinion and Informational Interdependence in the New Media Era." In *The Oxford Handbook of American Public Opinion and the Media*, ed. Robert Y. Shapiro, Lawrence R. Jacobs, and George C. Edwards III, 3–21. Oxford: Oxford University Press.

Jacobs, Lawrence, and Theda Skocpol, eds. 2005a. *Inequality and American Democracy: What We Know and What We Need to Learn*. New York: Sage.

————. 2005b. "Studying Inequality and American Democracy: Findings and Challenges." In *Inequality and American Democracy: What We Know and*

——. 2011. "Clarifying the Concept of Representation." *American Political Science Review* 105, no. 3:621–30.

Manza, Jeff, and Fay Lomax Cook. 2002a. "A Democratic Polity? Three Views of Policy Responsiveness to Public Opinion in the United States." *American Politics Research* 30, no. 6:630–67.

——. 2002b. "The Impact of Public Opinion on Public Policy: The State of the Debate." In *Navigating Public Opinion: Polls, Policy, and the Future of American Democracy*, ed. Jeff Manza, Fay Lomax Cook, and Benjamin I. Page, 17–32. New York: Oxford University Press.

March, James. 1999. *The Pursuit of Organizational Intelligence: Decisions and Learning in Organizations*. New York: Wiley-Blackwell.

Mayhew, David R. 1974. Congress: *The Electoral Connection*. New Haven, CT: Yale University Press.

McCall, Leslie. 2013. *The Undeserving Rich*. New York: Cambridge University Press.

McCarty, Nolan, Keith T. Poole, and Howard Rosenthal. 2005. *Polarized America: The Dance of Ideology and Unequal Riches*. Cambridge, MA: MIT Press.

McChesney, Fred. 1997. *Money for Nothing: Politicians, Rent Extraction, and Political Extortion*. Cambridge, MA: Harvard University Press.

McCombs, Maxwell E., and Donald L. Shaw. 1972. "The Agenda-Setting Function of Mass Media." *Public Opinion Quarterly* 36, no. 2:176–87.

——. 1993. "The Evolution of Agenda-Setting Research: Twenty-five Years in the Marketplace of Ideas." *Journal of Communication* 43 (Spring): 58–67.

McConnell, Grant. 1966. *Private Power and American Democracy*. New York: Knopf.

McCubbins, Matthew D., Roger G. Noll, and Barry Weingast. 1987. "Administrative Procedures as Instruments of Political Control." *Journal of Law, Economics, and Organization* 3, no. 2:243–77.

——. 1989. "Structure and Process, Politics and Policy: Administrative Arrangements and the Political Control of Agencies." *Virginia Law Review* 75:431–89.

Mendelsohn, Matthew. 1996. "The Media and Interpersonal Communication: The Priming of Issues, Leaders, and Party Identification." *Journal of Politics* 58, no. 1:112–25.

Merrill, Samuel, III, and Bernard Grofman. 1999. *A Unified Theory of Voting: Directional and Proximity Spatial Models*. Cambridge: Cambridge University Press.

Mettler, Suzanne, and Joe Soss. 2004. "The Consequences of Public Policy for Democratic Citizenship: Bridging Policy Studies and Mass Politics." *Perspectives on Politics* 1 (March): 55–73.

Michels, Robert. 1915/1962. *Political Parties: A Sociological Study of the Oligarchical Tendencies of Modern Democracy*. Translated by E. Paul and C. Paul. 2nd ed. New York: Free Press.

Miller, Arthur H., Martin P. Wattenberg, and Oksana Malanchuk. 1986. "Schematic Assessments of Presidential Candidates." *American Political Science Review* 80, no. 2 (June): 521–40.

Miller, Gary. 2005. "The Political Evolution of Principal-Agent Models." *Annual Review of Political Science* 8 (June): 203–25.

Miller, Joanne M., and Jon A. Krosnick. 1996. "News Media Impact on the Ingredients of Presidential Evaluations." In *Political Persuasion and Attitude Change*, ed. Diana C. Mutz, Paul M. Sniderman, and Richard A. Brody, 79–98. Ann Arbor: University of Michigan Press.

———. 2000. "News Media Impact on the Ingredients of Presidential Evaluations: Politically Knowledgeable Citizens Are Guided by a Trusted Source." *American Journal of Political Science* 44, no. 2:301–15.

Miller, Warren E., and Donald Stokes. 1963. "Constituency Influence in Congress." *American Political Science Review* 57:45–56.

Mills, C. Wright. 1956. *The Power Elite*. New York: Oxford University Press.

Moe, Terry M. 1985. "The Politicized Presidency." In *The New Directions in American Politics*, ed. John Chubb and Paul Peterson, 235–71. Washington, DC: Brookings Institution.

———. 1987. "An Assessment of the Positive Theory of 'Congressional Dominance.'" *Legislative Studies Quarterly* 12, no. 4:475–520.

———. 1993. "Presidents, Institutions and Theory." In *Researching the Presidency*, ed. George Edwards, John Kessel, and Bert Rockman, 337–86. Pittsburgh: University of Pittsburgh Press.

———. 2003. "The Presidency and the Bureaucracy: The Presidential Advantage." In *The Presidency and the Political System* (7th ed.), ed. Michael Nelson, 425–57. Washington, DC: Congressional Quarterly Press.

Monroe, Alan D. 1979. "Consistency between Policy Preferences and National Policy Decisions." *American Politics Quarterly* 7, no. 1:3–18.

———. 1998. "Public Opinion and Public Policy, 1980–1993." *Public Opinion Quarterly* 62, no. 1:6–28.

Morton Rebecca. 1993. "Incomplete Information and Ideological Explanations of Platform Divergence." *American Political Science Review* 87:382–92.

Murray, Shoon. 2006. "Private Polls and Presidential Policy Making: Reagan as Facilitator of Change." *Public Opinion Quarterly* 70:477–98.

Murray, Shoon, and Peter Howard. 2002. "Variation in White House Polling Operations: Carter to Clinton." *Public Opinion Quarterly* 66:527–58.

Mutz, D. C. 2006. *Hearing the Other Side: Deliberative versus Participatory Democracy*. New York: Cambridge University Press.

Mutz, Diana, and Jeffery J. Mondak. 1997. "Dimensions of Sociotropic Behavior: Group-Based Judgments of Fairness and Well-Being." *American Journal of Political Science* 41 (January): 284–308.

Mutz, D. C., and B. Reeves. 2005. "The New Videomalaise: Effects of Televised Incivility on Political Trust." *American Political Science Review* 99, no. 1:2–15.

Strolovitch, Dara. 2007. *Affirmative Advocacy: Race, Class, and Gender in Interest Group Politics*. Chicago: University of Chicago Press.

Taber, Charles, and Milton Lodge. 2006. "Motivated Skepticism in the Evaluation of Political Beliefs." *American Journal of Political Science* 50 (July): 755–69.

Tedin, Kent, Brandon Rottinghaus, and Harrell Rodgers. 2011. "When the President Goes Public: The Consequences of Communication Mode for Opinion Change across Issue Types and Groups." *Political Research Quarterly* 64, no. 3: 506–19.

Tett, Gillian. 2010. *Fool's Gold: The Inside Story of J. P. Morgan and How Wall St. Greed Corrupted Its Bold Dream and Created a Financial Catastrophe*. New York: Free Press.

Tomz, Michael, Jason Wittenberg, and Gary King. 2003. *CLARIFY: Software for Interpreting and Presenting Statistical Results*. Version 2.1. Stanford University, University of Wisconsin, and Harvard University, January 5. Available at http://gking.harvard.edu.

Traugott, Michael W., and Paul J. Lavrakas. 1996/2000. *The Voter's Guide to Election Polls*. 2nd ed. New York: Chatham House.

Truman, David. 1951. *The Governmental Process*. New York: Knopf.

Tulis, Jeffrey. 1987. *The Rhetorical Presidency*. Princeton, NJ: Princeton University Press.

Vaughan, Diane. 1997. *The Challenger Launch Decision: Risky Technology, Culture, and Deviance at NASA*. Chicago: University of Chicago Press.

Verba, Sidney, Kay Schlozman, and Henry Brady. 1995. *Voice and Equality: Civic Voluntarism in American Politics*. Cambridge, MA: Harvard University Press.

Visser, Penny S., George Y. Bizer, and Jon A. Krosnick. 2006. "Exploring the Latent Structure of Strength-Related Attitude Attributes." In *Advances in Experimental Social Psychology*, ed. Mark P. Zanna, 1–67. San Diego, CA: Academic.

Volcker, Paul. 2005. "An Economy on Thin Ice." *Washington Post*, April 10.

Weber, Max. 1978. *Economy and Society*. Translated by G. Roth. Berkeley and Los Angeles: University of California Press.

Weissberg, Robert. 1978. "Collective vs. Dynamic Representation in Congress." *American Political Science Review* 72:535–47.

West, Darrell M. 1988. "Activists and Economic Policymaking in Congress." *American Journal of Political Science* 32:662–80.

Westen, Drew. 2011. "What Happened to Obama? An Opinion Piece." *Political Science Quarterly* 126, no. 3:493–99.

Wildavsky, Aaron. 1964. *The Politics of the Budgetary Process*. Boston: Little, Brown.

Will, George. 2007. "Democratic Pandering to the Middle Class." *Washington Post*, October 17, 2007.

———. 2014. "Judicial Activism Isn't a Bad Thing." *Washington Post*, January 22.

Wilson, Woodrow. 1908. *Constitutional Government in the United States*. New York: Columbia University Press.

Winter, David G. 1987. "Leader Appeal, Leader Performance, and the Motive Profiles of Leaders and Followers." *Journal of Personality and Social Psychology* 52, no. 1:196–202.

Wirtz, James. 1991. *The Tet Offensive: Intelligence Failure in War*. Ithaca, NY: Cornell University Press.

Wlezien, Christopher. 2004. "Patterns of Representation: Dynamics of Public Preferences and Policy." *Journal of Politics* 66:1–24.

Wood, B. Dan. 2009. *The Myth of Presidential Representation*. New York: Cambridge University Press.

Wood, Gordon. 1969. *The Creation of the American Republic*. Chapel Hill: University of North Carolina Press.

Woodward, Bob. 2006. *State of Denial: Bush at War, Part III*. New York: Simon & Schuster.

Wright, Donald, and Timothy R. Reese. 2008. *On Point II: Transition to the New Campaign—the United States Army in Operation Iraqi Freedom*. Fort Leavenworth, KS: Combat Studies Institute Press.

Wright, Gerald C. 1989. "Policy Voting in the U.S. Senate: Who Is Represented?" *Legislative Studies Quarterly* 14 (November): 465–86.

Wright, John R. 1989. "PAC Contributions, Lobbying, and Representation." *Journal of Politics* 51, no. 3:713–29.

Young, Iris. 2000. *Inclusion and Democracy*. Oxford: Oxford University Press.

Young, Marilyn. 1991. *The Vietnam Wars, 1945–1990*. New York: Harper Collins.

Zaller, John. 1992. *The Nature and Origins of Mass Opinion*. New York: Cambridge University Press.

Chong, Dennis: on impact of media, 13, 131; on manipulation, 104, 105, 106, 111; on priming, 14, 15, 131

Clinton, William (Bill), xii, 19, 117, 122

Cohen, Jeffrey, 15, 37, 100, 106, 127

collective studies, 6

Congress (US), 55; Democrats in, ix; Republicans in, ix

Cook, Fay Lomax, 3, 45, 130, 131, 135–36

Cook, Thomas, 20

crafted talk, 12, 13, 76, 134; elite crafting, 61, 98; presidential crafting, 21, 37, 44, 50, 74, 91

Crete, Jean, 75, 127

Dahl, Robert: on elite governance, xiii–xvi, 3, 5, 71; on pluralism, 71, 133; on polyarchy, 120, 134–37. See also pluralism; polyarchy

Deaver, Michael, 27. See also Baker, James; Meese, Edwin

Delli Carpini, Michael, 65, 135–36

Democratic Party, 35, 62–64, 70, 98; Catholic coalition and, 35, 62–65, 67, 69; New Deal coalition and, 62–63, 65, 124

Dempsey, Glen, 15, 106

DeRouen, Karl, Jr., 77

Dewey, John, 135

Disch, Lisa, 136; on dyadic representation, 3, 6; on elite influence, 61, 97–98, 128–32; on manipulation, 97; on responsiveness, 6, 128, 130; on symbolic representation, 3, 8

Downs, Anthony, 3, 5, 71, 128, 133; median voter theory, 5, 9, 133

Druckman, James, 26, 134, 135, 136; on dyadic representation, 9; on framing, 92, 131; on impact of media, 15, 131; on issue priming, 13, 14, 75, 92, 127, 131; on manipulation, 14, 98, 104, 105, 106, 111, 132; on presidential image, 76, 77. See also priming

Edelman, Murray, 8. See also representation: symbolic

Edsall, Mary, 62

Edsall, Thomas Byrne, 62

Edwards, George, III, 15, 22, 82, 103–4, 115, 116, 126, 127, 130, 131; on elites, 15; on framing, 131; on issue priming, 131; on presidential polling, 22; on presidential

response to public opinion, 82. See also manipulation

Ehrlichman, John, 58

Eisinger, Robert, on presidential polling methods, 17, 19, 22–23, 45, 55, 85, 87, 122. See also presidential poll

electoral college, xiv, 60

elites, xvi, xviii, 15, 136; antielites, xviii; competition between, 133–37; governing elites, xi–xii, xiii–xvii, 5; impact of, xvii, 10, 11, 13–16, 97, 111, 115, 118, 129, 131; independence of, xv, xviii; manipulation by, 98–99, 104, 105, 106, 126, 129, 131–32; mobilization and, 74–75; scheme of representation and, 20; strategies of, 7, 13, 71, 74–75, 80, 92–93, 119–20, 129–33. See also salience

Enelow, James, 13

Enns, Peter, 61

Erikson, Robert, 9, 61, 123; on responsiveness, 5, 6, 7, 12, 18, 39, 44, 48, 68, 73

Eulau, Heinz, 128

Executive Office of the President, 12–13

Fearon, James, 73, 125

Feaver, Peter, 105

Federalist Papers, xiv, 14, 60

Federal Reserve Bank, xii, xv, xvi–xvii

Fein, Jordan, 14, 135

Fenno, Richard, 77

Ferejohn, John, 6

Ferguson, Leroy, 128

Fernandes, Juliana, 111

Fetlock, Philip, 13

Fisher, Louis, 105

Fiske, Susan, 34, 76

Fleisher, Richard, 104

Foyle, Douglas, 77, 105

framing, 13, 14, 15, 103, 105, 136–37; counterframing, 15, 105–6, 134; elite framing, 129, 131; presidential framing, 92. See also Druckman, James; priming

Friedman, Thomas, ix, xi

Fung, Archon, 136

Funk, Carolyn, 34, 76

Gabel, Matthew, 14, 103

Garsten, Bryan, 119, 132

Geer, John, 17, 45, 55, 76

Gelpi, Christopher, 105

Gerber, Alan, 111, 137

Gerring, John, xv, 60, 125
Gilens, Martin, xvii, 10, 61, 72, 124
Gimpel, James, 111
Goldwater, Barry, 62
Gordon, Michael, xii
Great Depression, ix, xii. *See also* Democratic Party: New Deal coalition and
Green, Donald, 105, 111, 137
Greenspan, Alan, xvi–xvii
Groeling, Tim, 106
Gronke, Paul, 6–7

Haberman, Maggie, 123
Habermas, Jürgen, 7, 97, 129–30
Hacker, Jacob, xii, xvii, 72, 124, 133
Haldeman, H. R., 24, 26–27, 57, 81. *See also* Nixon, Richard
Hamilton, Alexander, xiv
Hammond, Thomas, 32
Harpham, Edward, xviii
Harris, Louis, 23, 25. *See also* Quayle, Oliver
Heith, Dianne, on presidential polling, 17, 19, 22–23, 45, 122. *See also* presidential poll
Held, David, 3
Herman, Edward, 14, 97
Herron, Michael, xv
Hill, Kim Quaile, 6, 105
Hinich, Melvin, 13
Holmes, Justin, 75, 77, 104, 106, 127
Holsti, Ole, 105
Horkheimer, Max, 97–98
Howard, Peter, 18, 19, 122
Huckfeldt, Robert, 105
Humes, Brian, 32
Hurley, Patricia, 6. *See also* representation: dyadic
Hurwitz, Jon, 15, 104

ideological identification. *See* lumping
inequality, 72; demands of the privileged and, xvii, 4, 35, 124, 135; economic segmentation and, 4, 10, 11, 35, 61, 72, 124. *See also* representation: segmented
iron law of oligarchy, xviii. *See also* Michels, Robert
Iyengar, Shanto, 45; on image priming, 76, 77, 79, 81; on impact of the media, 13; on issue priming, 75; on presidential personality, 34

Jackson, Melinda, 24, 26
Jacobs, Lawrence, 11, 37, 117, 124, 133, 135–36; on dyadic representation, 9; on economic segmentation, 4, 10, 35; on elite effectiveness, xvi, xviii, 10, 16, 131, 136; on framing, 131; on image priming, 77, 78, 122; on issue priming, 76, 127, 131; on manipulation, 98, 99, 104, 105, 126, 130, 131; on persuasion, 115; on presidential polling procedures, 19, 22, 23, 24, 26, 28, 33, 55, 101, 122; on responsiveness, xvii, 11, 16–17, 38, 45, 124; on segmentation, 61, 72, 124
Jacoby, William, 22, 32, 75, 127
Jerit, Jennifer, 104
Job, Brian, 77
Johnson, Lyndon: manipulation by, 98, 100–111, 126; polling and, 24, 25, 39, 101–3, 108, 111, 118; presidential performance of, 107; priming and, 100, 106–7, 112–14, 116, 126
Johnson, Paul, 105
Johnston, Richard, 75, 127

Keeter, Scott, 65
Kennedy, Edward, image priming and, 81
Kennedy, John F.: manipulation by, 98; polling and, 23, 25. *See also* Harris, Louis
Kernell, Samuel, 28, 37, 60
Kiewiet, Roderick, 61
Kim, Dukhong, 130
Kinder, Donald: on image priming, 76, 77, 78–79, 81; on impact of the media, 13; on issue priming, 75; on presidential personality, 34; on voting behavior, 61
King, Anthony, 4, 12
King, Desmond, xvii
King, Gary, 19, 20, 22
Kingdon, John, 44, 123
Kirsch, Richard, 136
Koh, Harold, 82
Kraft, John, 24, 25. *See also* Napolitan, Joseph; Quayle, Oliver
Krosnick, Jon, 45; on elite mobilization, 15; on image priming, 74, 76, 78, 81; on issue approval (policy position), 31; on manipulation, 104; on presidential image, 34
Kuklinski, James, 13

Lau, Richard, 34, 76
Lavrakas, Paul, 32

Lazarsfeld, Paul, 75, 127
Leeper, Thomas, 14, 135
Lemert, James, 33
Lippmann, Walter, xv
Lodge, Milton, 15, 104, 131, 135
Lowi, Theodore, 132
lumping, 8, 30–31, 43, 44, 45, 46, 47, 48, 50, 52, 67, 121, 123. *See also* presidential poll: lumping
Lupia, Arthur, 13, 15, 106

MacKuen, Michael, 123; on dyadic representation, 9, 61; on polling methods, 22; on responsiveness, 5, 6, 7, 12, 18, 39, 44, 48, 68, 73
Madison, James, xiv, xvii, 9, 12
Malanchuk, Oksana, 34, 76–77
Mandelbaum, Michael, ix, xi
Manin, Bernard, 7, 61
manipulation, 14, 98, 100–104, 116, 126, 127, 131
Mansbridge, Jane, 8, 60, 98, 116, 124, 128–29
Manza, Jeff, 3, 7, 45
March, James, xvii
Market Opinion Research, 24, 25
Mayhew, David, 3, 73
McAvoy, Gregory, 38
McCall, Leslie, 136
McCarty, Nolan, 10
McChesney, Fred, 4, 11, 122
McConnell, Grant, xviii, 71
McCubbins, Matthew, 125
McGraw, Kathleen, 131
McIver, John, 7
McPhee, William, 75, 127
media, 101, 122; political impact of, 13, 15, 19, 37, 97, 105, 111, 114, 131; social media, 19
median voter theory, 5, 9, 10, 11, 133. *See also* voters
Medicare, x, xii
Meese, Edwin, 27. *See also* Baker, James; Deaver, Michael
Mendelsohn, Matthew, 32, 76
Mertz, Robert, 33
Mettler, Suzanne, 130
Michels, Robert, xviii
Miller, Arthur, 34, 76–77,
Miller, Gary, 73, 125
Miller, Joanne, 31, 34; on priming, 74, 76, 78, 81

Miller, Warren, 6, 9, 61, 124
Mills, C. Wright, xviii, 71, 132
Moe, Terry, xv, 9, 23, 60, 71, 102, 125
Mondak, Jeffery, 61
Monroe, Alan, 7, 45
mood, 7, 44–45, 46, 70, 102, 106. *See also* Stimson, James
Moyers, Bill, 101, 102
Mulroy, Quinn, xv, 60, 125
Murray, Shoon, 18, 19, 122, 123
Mutz, Diana, 61, 105

Napolitan, Joseph, 24, 25. *See also* Kraft, John; Quayle, Oliver
National Commission on the Causes of the Financial and Economic Crisis in the United States 2011, xii, xvi, xvii
national health insurance. *See* Affordable Care Act (ACA)
Nelson, Thomas, 13. *See also* priming
Nincic, Miroslav, 77
Nixon, Richard, 8, 11, 22, 28, 59; domestic issues and, 53–54, 87, 92, 126; foreign issues and, 53–54, 79, 80, 87, 88; framing and, 92; polling and, 24, 25, 33, 39, 47, 48, 49, 50, 51, 52, 57–59, 85, 121; presidential performance of, 26, 79–81, 83–84, 86, 88–90, 92; priming and, 80, 81, 87, 90, 92, 126; Vietnam War and, 39, 54, 57, 74, 79–80, 85, 88, 92, 126. *See also* China; Teeter, Robert
Noll, Roger, 125
North, Douglass, 23

Obama, Barack, xii, 100, 134; administration of, 123. *See also* Affordable Care Act (ACA)
Olson, Mancur, 133, 136
Opinion Research Corporation, 24, 25
Ostermeier, Eric, 26, 38
Ostrom, Charles, 77
Oxley, Zoe, 13. *See also* priming

Page, Benjamin, 21, 22, 34, 59, 75, 123, 127; on demands of the privileged, xvii, 4, 35, 124, 135; on dyadic responsiveness, 6; on economic segmentation, 10, 61, 72, 124; on image building as strategy, 21, 22, 59, 76; on impact of the media, 135; on manipulation, 98, 105, 106, 130; on median voters, 9; on persuasion, 115; on presidential performance (approval), 15; on splitting (public policy preferences), 6, 8, 38, 45

Palmquist, Bradley, 105

Park, Jee-Kwang, 15, 104, 127

Peffley, Mark, 15, 104

persuasion, 14, 33, 40, 102, 106–7, 127; marginal, 114–16. *See also* manipulation

Peters, Mark, 34, 76

Petrocik, John, 22, 31, 65, 75, 127

Phillips, Kevin, xi, 57–58

Pierson, Paul, xii, xvii, 23, 72, 124, 133

Pitkin, Hannah, 5, 16, 124, 129, 138. *See also* representation: symbolic

Plotke, David, 129

pluralism, 71, 133. *See also* Dahl, Robert

polyarchy, 120, 128, 134–37. *See also* Dahl, Robert

Poole, Keith, 10

Popkin, Samuel, 76–77

Popper, Karl, 20

Powell, Lynda, 6

preferences. *See* presidential poll: of policy preferences

presidential poll, 23, 26, 27, 29, 30, 33, 37, 50, 121; of issue approval (policy position), 29, 31, 48, 51, 57, 66; lumping (ideological identification) and, 8, 30–31, 43, 44, 45, 46, 47, 48, 50, 52, 67, 121, 123; of most important problem, 29, 126–27; personality polls (image polls), 8, 28, 29, 33, 34, 59, 119, 121, 122; of policy preferences, 5, 28–30, 32, 33, 34, 39, 40, 71, 119, 121, 123; of presidential performance, 26, 29, 31, 34, 36, 79, 81, 83–84, 86, 88–92, 107; splitting (policy opinion) and, 30–31, 32, 43–44, 45, 46, 47, 48, 49, 50, 52, 55, 56, 64, 69, 123; subgroup demographics and, 29, 64–67. *See also* presidential polling attitudes; priming; representation; salience

presidential polling attitudes: pure lumping, 46, 48–49, 51; pure splitting, 46, 48–49

Prewett, Kenneth, 120

Price, Vincent, 105

priming, 13–14, 80, 106–9, 112, 120, 129, 131; constrained priming, 112–14; emphasis and, 38, 108, 112; image priming, 73–81, 83, 88, 90, 92, 116, 126; importance and, 108, 111–12. issue priming, 73–76, 80–83, 88, 92, 101, 119, 122; *See also* framing

Prior, Markus, 135

progressives, xii

*Public Opinion Quarterly*, 26

*Public Papers of the Presidents of the United States*, 38. See also *Weekly Compilation of Presidential Documents*

Quayle, Oliver, 24, 25, 101. *See also* Kraft, John; Napolitan, Joseph

Ragsdale, Lynn, 26

Raju, Manu, x

Reagan, Ronald, 11, 22, 28, 56, 70, 117, 124, 125; affluent interest of, 65, 68, 124; domestic policy and, 53–54; foreign policy and, 53–55, 79, 82, 87; framing and, 92; polling and, 24, 25, 34, 47–53, 56, 58–59, 61–70, 85, 121; presidential performance of, 26, 82–84, 86, 89; priming and, 79, 86–87, 90–92, 125. *See also* Wirthlin, Richard

Reese, Timothy, xii

Rehfeld, Andrew, 124

Reifler, Jason, 105

representation, 119, 124, 132, 138; collective, 6; dyadic, 6, 9, 60, 61; political, 21; principal-agent, 125–27; segmented, 10–11, 61, 64, 71–72, 120, 124; substantive, 8, 16, 20, 40; symbolic, 8

Republican Party, 55, 62–63, 65, 72, 98, 134; social conservatives and, 11, 35, 56, 59, 62, 69, 124

responsiveness, 3, 5, 40, 45, 119, 124, 125, 129, 138; delegate/trustee model of, 128–29

Ricks, Thomas, xii, 16

Riker, William, 22, 32, 37, 75, 78, 126, 127

Ripley, Brian, 118

Ripley, Randall, 133

Rodden, Jonathan, 5

Rodgers, Harrell, 15, 104, 127

Roosevelt, Franklin Delano (FDR), 11, 23

Roosevelt, Theodore (Teddy), xviii

Rosenberg, Robert, 6–7

Rosenthal, Howard, 10

Rottinghaus, Brandon, 15, 18, 19, 23, 45, 80, 82, 90, 99, 103, 104, 107, 115, 122, 123, 126, 127

Sagan, Scott, xvii

salience, 4, 21, 25, 29, 30, 43, 44, 45, 54, 56, 119, 121, 122, 123

Sandel, Michael, 60
Sartori, Giovanni, xv
Schandler, Herbert, 106
Schattschneider, E. E., xviii, 71, 132, 133, 136
Scheve, Kenneth, 14, 103
Schickler, Eric, 23, 105
Schlozman, Kay, 61, 136
Schudson, Michael, 105
Schumpeter, Joseph, xv, 133
Seidelman, Raymond, xviii
Sellers, Patrick, 34, 75, 76, 77, 127
Shadish, William, 20
Shapiro, Catherine, 6
Shapiro, Robert, 11, 119, 129, 130, 133, 135; on dyadic representation, 61; on elite effectiveness, 4, 11; on image priming, 77, 78, 122; on issue priming, 73, 75, 76, 127; on lumping (ideological identification), 123; on manipulation, 98, 99, 104, 105, 106, 126; on persuasion, 115; on presidential performance polling (approval), 15, 16, 22–23; on presidential personality, 37; on presidential polling, 17, 19, 22, 23, 24, 26, 55, 101, 122; on salience, 37; on splitting (public's policy preferences), 6, 7, 8, 45
Shaw, Daron, 111
Shear, Michael, 123
Shepsle, Kenneth, 21, 59
Shils, Edward, 93
shirking, 4, 21, 122, 127
Shotts, Kenneth, xv
Sigelman, Lee, 13
Skocpol, Theda, 136; on inequality, 10, 11, 72; on institutional design, xviii; on skepticism of the elites, xii; on the Tea Party, xii. See also Tea Party movement
Sniderman, Paul, 13
Snyder, James, 5
social media, 19, 135
Social Security, x, 65, 121; privatization of, 11, 58–59, 130
Soroka, Stuart, 3, 6, 22, 35, 45
Soss, Joe, 130
Sprague, John, 105
State of the Union (speech), 12, 103
Stimson, James, 123, 130; on dyadic approach, 9, 61; on lumping, 46; on polling methods, 22; on responsiveness, 5, 6, 7, 12, 18, 39, 44, 48, 68, 73

Stokes, Donald, 6, 9, 61, 124
Stone, Deborah, xvii, xvi
Stone, Walter, 6
Stroh, Patrick, 131
Strolovitch, Dara, 133
Sullivan, John, 105, 115

Taber, Charles, 15, 104, 135
Tea Party movement, x, xii. See also Skocpol, Theda
Tedin, Kent, 15, 104, 127
Teeter, Robert, 24, 28, 58, 90
Tett, Gillian, xvii
Tewksbury, David, 105
Theis, John, 26
Tierney, John, 136
Trainor, Bernard, xii
Traugott, Michael, 32
Truman, David, 133
Tulis, Jeffrey, xv, 60

University of Michigan's Institute for Social Research, 26
US Constitution, framing of the, xiv–xvi, xviii, 20, 60, 97

Vaughan, Diane, xvii
Verba, Sidney, 61, 136
Vietnam War. See Nixon, Richard: Vietnam War and
Visser, Penny, 15, 104
Volcker, Paul, xi
voters: independent voters, 61, 62, 63, 65, 67, 68; median voters, 3, 5, 10–11, 30, 34, 51, 56, 59, 71, 119, 128, 130; responsiveness to, 11, 30, 130; swing voters (split ticket voters), 28, 40, 44, 50, 56, 57, 58, 59, 64, 65, 121; undecided voters, 11

Wahlke, John, 128
Wattenberg, Martin, 34, 76–77
Weber, Max, 130
Weekly Compilation of Presidential Documents, 38. See also Public Papers of the Presidents of the United States
Weingast, Barry, 125
Weissberg, Robert, 7
West, Darrell, 10
Westen, Drew, 74
Wildavsky, Aaron, 39, 48
Will, George, xvi

Williamson, Vanessa, xii
Wilson, Woodrow, 9
Winter, David, 78, 79
Wirthlin, Richard, 24, 26, 28, 58, 63–64,
    80–81, 87; Decision Making Informa-
    tion (Inc.) and, 24, 25. *See also* Reagan,
    Ronald: polling and
Wirtz, James, 106
Wlezien, Christopher, 3, 6, 22, 35, 43,
    45, 61

Wood, B. Dan, xvii, 3, 10, 34, 61, 124, 133
Wood, Gordon, xiv, 60
Woodward, Bob, xii
Wright, Donald, xii
Wright, Gerald, 7, 10, 45

Young, Iris, 129
Young, Marilyn, 79, 105, 117

Zaller, John, 13, 14, 103, 111

# Chicago Studies in American Politics

A SERIES EDITED BY BENJAMIN I. PAGE, SUSAN HERBST,
LAWRENCE R. JACOBS, AND ADAM J. BERINSKY

*Series titles, continued from front matter:*

ELECTING JUDGES: THE SURPRISING EFFECTS
OF CAMPAIGNING ON JUDICIAL LEGITIMACY
*by James L. Gibson*

FOLLOW THE LEADER? HOW VOTERS
RESPOND TO POLITICIANS' POLICIES AND
PERFORMANCE *by Gabriel S. Lenz*

THE SOCIAL CITIZEN: PEER NETWORKS AND
POLITICAL BEHAVIOR *by Betsy Sinclair*

THE SUBMERGED STATE: HOW INVISIBLE
GOVERNMENT POLICIES UNDERMINE AMERICAN
DEMOCRACY *by Suzanne Mettler*

DISCIPLINING THE POOR: NEOLIBERAL
PATERNALISM AND THE PERSISTENT POWER OF
RACE *by Joe Soss, Richard C. Fording, and
Sanford F. Schram*

WHY PARTIES? A SECOND LOOK *by
John H. Aldrich*

NEWS THAT MATTERS: TELEVISION AND
AMERICAN OPINION, UPDATED EDITION *by
Shanto Iyengar and Donald R. Kinder*

SELLING FEAR: COUNTERTERRORISM, THE MEDIA,
AND PUBLIC OPINION *by Brigitte L. Nacos,
Yaeli Bloch-Elkon, and Robert Y. Shapiro*

OBAMA'S RACE: THE 2008 ELECTION AND THE
DREAM OF A POST-RACIAL AMERICA *by Michael
Tesler and David O. Sears*

FILIBUSTERING: A POLITICAL HISTORY OF
OBSTRUCTION IN THE HOUSE AND SENATE
*by Gregory Koger*

IN TIME OF WAR: UNDERSTANDING AMERICAN
PUBLIC OPINION FROM WORLD WAR II TO
IRAQ *by Adam J. Berinsky*

US AGAINST THEM: ETHNOCENTRIC
FOUNDATIONS OF AMERICAN OPINION
*by Donald R. Kinder and Cindy D. Kam*

THE PARTISAN SORT: HOW LIBERALS BECAME
DEMOCRATS AND CONSERVATIVES BECAME
REPUBLICANS *by Matthew Levendusky*

DEMOCRACY AT RISK: HOW TERRORIST THREATS
AFFECT THE PUBLIC *by Jennifer L. Merolla and
Elizabeth J. Zechmeister*

AGENDAS AND INSTABILITY IN AMERICAN
POLITICS, SECOND EDITION *by Frank R.
Baumgartner and Bryan D. Jones*

THE PRIVATE ABUSE OF THE PUBLIC
INTEREST *by Lawrence D. Brown and
Lawrence R. Jacobs*

THE PARTY DECIDES: PRESIDENTIAL
NOMINATIONS BEFORE AND AFTER REFORM
*by Marty Cohen, David Karol, Hans Noel, and
John Zaller*

SAME SEX, DIFFERENT POLITICS: SUCCESS
AND FAILURE IN THE STRUGGLES OVER GAY
RIGHTS *by Gary Mucciaroni*